POETRY ANTHOLOGY

Written By

NORTHAMPTONSHIRE SCHOOLCHILDREN

Napier Nationwide Limited.
3 Fieldhouse Road, Rochdale, OL12 0AD.
Telephone: 01706 869654.

Published – 1995 by Napier Nationwide Ltd.

ISBN 1-86142-003-X

Typesetting, Design & Artwork by David Newton.
Phototypeset in 11/14pt Souvenir Medium & Demi.

To Jack

FOREWORD

It gives me great pleasure to provide a foreword to this anthology of poetry written by pupils from Northamptonshire primary schools. I am sure that everyone who reads this book will be delighted by the range and freshness of the children's work. Poetry allows the writer to capture the moment, to share experiences, to reflect on thoughts, dreams and real issues, and to craft language in powerful ways.

It is important children view themselves, from an early age, as real writers. This volume will reach a wide and enthusiastic audience and will provide the poets with a tremendous stimulus to continue exploring language and ideas. I hope this anthology brings you many hours of pleasurable reading.

Tony Drane
General Education Inspector

CONTENTS

A DAY TRIP

The coach ride was tedious,
We finally reached
LONDON!
Everyone climbed out of the coach.
We walked into a colossal building,
Absolutely amazing,
The galleries were unbelievable.
First the ecology section,
It was really colourful and interesting,
The sun was like a red hot fire.
Then there were the dinosaurs,
They looked monstrous and realistic,
They were massive,
And finally human biology,
Fascinating, funny,
Mirrors that made your body look small
And your head look like a sausage.
My favourite bit was entrance to the ecology,
As I walked through it,
It made me feel like I was in a real jungle!
On the way home Sarah and I played draughts,
Chess, snap and Master Mind.
I really enjoyed my trip to the Natural History Museum!

Amy Stuart (10)
Whitefriars Junior School

A JOURNEY ON A BIKE

I heave up Cart Hill,
I struggle to move,
My legs ache and climb.
The steep hill will not let me reach the summit,
I fiddle with my gears,
I try and try,
I have to put my foot down.

Timothy Smith (8)
Barby CE Primary School

PLAYING IN THE SNOW

When I was out with my friend Andy
There was a big white sheet of snow.
When I went out with my friend Andy
We went to the fields
Where the cold winds blow.
We went to the big white arch way
And played on the icing cake.
Then when I looked around the big white sheet
The world was full of flakes.

Jack Woodcock (9)
Newnham Primary School

RIDING

When you ride a bike
Muscles ache
Pushing on pedals
Up a hill.
Tired and sweaty,
Your face is bright red
And straggly hair
Is sticking to your face.

Tammi Gordon (10)
South End Junior School

THE FAIR

I like it when we go to the fair
Because you can buy candyfloss there.
I like it when we go on the big wheel
Because I think you get a good deal.

Although I'm afraid of heights
I love going to the big wheel on late nights.
I also like it when I go up and down
And even when I can nearly touch the ground.
My favourite weather I like at the fair is sun,
Because I know I can have lots of fun.

Gemma Lindsell (11)
Long Buckby Junior School

A DAY BY THE SEA

Sand on the beach,
Sand in the sea,
Sand can be fun for you or me.

Look at the waves crashing to the ground
Washing up shells ready to be found.
As I hear the chiming of a clock
A wave crashes onto a rock.

Sand on the beach, sunshine too,
Cuckoos in the background, cuckoo, cuckoo!

Sand on the beach,
Sand in the sea,
Sand is fun for you and me.

Harriet Becker-Ging (10)
Long Buckby Junior School

MY PIANO LESSON

On my first lesson I learned the notes,
Next week I hopped the octave.
On my third lesson I stayed to lunch,
Next week it's these notes GBDFA,
But I say Great Big Dog Fighting Auntie.
Fifth week I learn a song, Twinkle Twinkle Little Star.
Next week I sleep at my piano teacher's house,
My brother got jealous because I got three lessons.

Jocelyn Garner (8)
Cedar Road Lower School

GOING SHOPPING

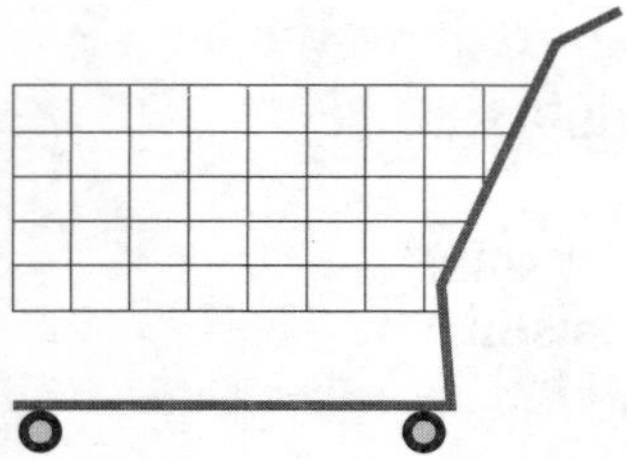

Get the trolley,
Put the pound in,
Get the cat food,
Get the crisps,
Get everything
And queue, and queue,
And queue.

Leah Kikta (7)
Cedar Road Lower School

SPEED BOAT

When I get in my speed boat
I turn the engine on and shout "Hurray! Here I come."
The waves splash against the sides,
The water turns to froth,
Oh, how much fun I have in my little white speedboat.

Robert Morgan (8)
Cedar Road Lower School

FISHING

When you fish you use a rod,
When you fish you can catch a cod,
But first of all you'll need some bait,
Hopefully the fish will put it on a plate.

Then you'll need a long bit of line,
Hopefully it will be fine.
Of course you'll have to have some skill
If you don't catch anything don't use a drill.
But soon you'll catch nine or ten
Soon you'll be as good as them

Mark Scoble (9)
Long Buckby Junior School

GO-KARTING

Racing round the circuit
As the dust spurts into the air.

I hear another kart
So I thrust the pedal to the metal.

The g-force pushes my head to the head rest
As the stench of fuel is propelled into the air.

Mark Williams (9)
Barby CE Primary School

BIKE RIDE

"Come on Becky, it's dinner time",
"I'm coming mum",
"It's a horrible day, isn't it kids?"
"Yes it is dad",
"Dad I don't like peas",
"Try and eat some please",
"I've finished dad",
"Oh look the rain's cleared up now
We can go for a bike ride",
"But mum!"
"Go and get some old clothes on you two",
"But I want to go in these clothes or I'm not coming!"
"Come on then Becky, we've got a big hill to get up now",
"I can't get up it, I'm going to push my bike up",
"Ha ha! Becky can't get up the hill!"
"Shut up Daniel",
"Help mum I'm going backwards!"
"Look who's talking Daniel!"
"Shut up Becky!"
"Oh, no! It's started to sleet",
"Dad, it keeps going in my eyes",
"Push your bike then, Becky",
Hhmmmm!
"Oh dad I don't like thunder".
We're in Byfield now at our doorstep.
"I didn't like that bike ride",
"Becky is a scaredy cat!"
"Shut up Daniel!"
"Mum I didn't like that bike ride,
I'd rather have stayed at home".

Becky Goswell (9)
Byfield Primary School

SCRAMBLING ON MY QUAD

The quiet engine starts revving up,
I slowly ease my big black helmet on,
I slam the visor down.
I quickly click the bike into reverse,
The field is lying in front of me,
Beckoning me, saying come and ride over me.
I zoom through the air,
The pond comes into sight.
The snow leaps up onto my back.
Wetness seeps through my clothes.
I gradually switch the gears down,
I am home.

Richard Williams (9)
Barby CE Primary School

A CHRISTINGLE SERVICE

Half past six,
Christingle service.
I went into the church,
I was given a Christingle.
It was an orange,
Strange.
We sang songs, hymns,
Mrs Turnbull said a poem,
The Rector said a prayer.
My brother said he fell asleep
But I didn't really care.

James Clews (9)
Barby CE Primary School

THE ROYAL WHALE

The Royal Whale,
A monster of the sea,
A royal beauty.
Talks to his friends
In his booming
Echo talk.
A swimming king,
Swims to his palace.
A fat heavy
Disturbs the shining surface.
Now a net of many squares
Dragged the big load of blubber
To lard.
The dead, once king, is sawn through
With a powerful hand saw.
Pink meat fall to the grey floor,
Not grey but red with blood.
The teeth fall to the floor,
The heart is ripped from the body,
And pounding it fall to the floor,
The once mighty ruler
Is a pile of flesh, blood
And gut.

Joanne Hyslop (10)
Whitefriars Junior School

POLAR BEAR

Polar bears are strong
But why do we kill them,
Open to the world.
Lives on the wild.
A polar bear lives free
Remember the polar bear.

Be kind to polar bears
Extinct nearly.
Are you a killer?
Remind people of the polar bear.

Richard MacLennan (7)
Rectory Farm Lower School

WIGGLY SNAKE

Wiggly snake climbing up my tree.
Whack it once, whack it twice,
Shall I wait for the snake
To come down from the tree.
No I won't wait for the snake
To come down from the tree
Because it will wiggle
After me.

Matthew Hawker (6)
Lewis De Haan (7)
Waynflete Infant School

HORSES

I like horses because
You can ride on them
And it is fun.
I like it very much,
It makes me feel happy.
I like them because
They are sometimes smooth
And they have lovely long tails
And they have massive eyes as well.

Claire Allen (6)
Natalia Harrison (7)
Waynflete Infant School

THE HUNTER

The hunter coming from behind.
Prey not noticing the shadow creeping over it.
Hunter looking from side to side very quietly.
Prey notices, runs for cover.
Hunter pouncing, again and again,
But misses every time.
At last prey is caught.
The weasel had its dinner.

Kimberley Dudley (7)
Southfield Primary School

ANIMAL RHYMES

In our bath I've got a whale,
It knocked my mum out with its tail.

In my room I've got a leopard,
It got out one day and ate the shepherd.

In our hall I've got a lion,
My mum went mad when he ate our iron.

In my shed I've got a pig,
He lost his hair and now wears a wig!

In my tree there is a bird,
He'll never ever say a word.

In the lounge there is my panther,
"He'll eat you up" says Samantha.

In the spare room there is a fox,
He sleeps in the TV box.

In the bathroom there's a kangaroo,
He sleeps on the floor and lives in the loo.

In the front room there is a bear,
My dad went wild when he broke the chair.

In the fridge I had a spider,
But on Christmas Eve he drowned in cider.

Adam Cowland (10)
South End Junior School

DOGS

Dogs are born
Then they go to a shop.
Someone buys one.
The dog gets a bowl,
Then it gets a home.
It grows bigger,
Then it might win.
The Crufts dog show,
It will be famous too.

Lynsey Walsh (6)
Redwell Infant School

THE ANIMAL SONG
Tigers go arr!
And monkeys go a a a a!
And horses go nay
So lets sing an animal song.
Madison Brooks (6)
Waynflete Infant School

NONSENSE
The moo cowed,
The baa sheeped,
The quack ducked,
The oink pigged,
The farmer walked backwards
And wondered why.

The next morning
The cow went moo,
The sheep went baa,
The duck went quack,
The pig went oink,
The farmer walked forward
And jumped for joy.
Everything was back to normal.
Sarah Cumberpatch (9)
Weedon Bec Primary School

SNAKE
Snakes change,
They start off as eggs,
Then the eggs crack,
A snake comes out,
They've got white skin,
They are little,
They grow bigger.
Aaron Merricks (7)
Redwell Infant School

ZEBRAS
Zebras are horses
Hiding in between
Strips of leaves
Watching for
The sun coloured lion.
Charlotte Ferguson (6)
Weedon Bec Primary School

AN ALLITERATION POEM

One white whale waiting.
Two squirrels serving sausages.
Three seals slowly swimming.
Four nasty newts nosing.
Five foxes falling fast.
Six apes eating apples.
Seven tangled thrushes in thorns.
Eight terrapins terrifying tadpoles.
Nine fish fighting other fish.
Ten wolves washing in water.

Wayne Fuller (8)
Newton Road Junior School

THE TIGER

Tigers are born to be free.
In zoos they should not be there.
Great beasts they are.
Eats on meat.
Not their fault.
Remember the tiger.

Scott Boswell (8)
Rectory Farm Lower School

WHALE

Why are whales being killed?
Have you any care?
Another being killed each day.
Live to be free.
Extinct soon if this carries on.

Mark Smith (8)
Rectory Farm Lower School

TIGER, TIGER

The tiger looks at you with a cold stare.
Then he roars.
He walks distinguished.
Like a famous movie star.
His skin so beautiful
That man will kill for it.
Then he sees a baby water hog,
He pounds he slashes at you
With a sickle for a claw.
He's always on the move
Like a robot out of control.
He wanders around the jungle
Like a little toy soldier.
He hears a bullet coming towards him
Like an axe splitting a log.
And bang! He's dead
Like a dormant temple.

Thomas Spencer (11)
Newton Road Junior School

THE LEAN MEAN FIGHTING MACHINE

Tiger: pounding like a working machine.
Luminous eyes like a burning crackling fire.
Teeth as sharp as a knife.
Respectable like a jewel in a museum.
Monstrous growl roars out loud.
Nearly makes your shoes lift off the ground.
Frightening face like a greyhound.
Enormous paws like a football.
Stalks in.
Vivid.
Stripes.

Jodie Cooper (11)
Newton Road Junior School

TIGER DAYS TIGER WAYS

Tigers hunt their victims
From Antelopes to Zebras.
He camouflages himself
Like a chameleon on a palisade.
The tiger is a carnivore,
He loves devouring animals
And after he becomes informally listless.
Although the tiger is vicious
He is an endangered species,
The tiger is glorious in many ways.

Matthew Davis (11)
Newton Road Junior School

A CINQUAIN

Horse
Big, fast
Can canter, gallop, walk
I like them
Mare.

Emma-Jane Borowski (8)
Newton Road Junior School

THE TIGER

He stalks his prey to capture and kill.
He's nimble on his feet like a ballerina.
He should be king of the jungle
But the lion took his place.
He's not a publicity seeker.
He's one of the shyest of felines.
He's speedy like the greatest car
And his teeth are like razors.
He's stripy like a hefty wasp
This is the tiger.

Dale Brunton (11)
Newton Road Junior School

TIGER POEM

The tiger, teeth like razors,
The tiger, eyes blazing,
The tiger, nose picking up scent,
The tiger, ears twitching,
The tiger, claws sinking in the soft ground.

Adrenalin running wild in his body,
His legs charged with energy.
Suddenly rip roaring speed,
Then stop.
He hears something,
His stripes like army camouflage.

He is stalking, waiting for the right moment.
He walks through his jungle home
As a king should,
Jumping over logs and low vines.

Mark Chapman (10)
Newton Road Junior School

LION

Lions are becoming extinct.
I wish lions would live in the wild.
Only to be so free and happy.
No hunters should kill lions.

Shannon Eaglestone (8)
Rectory Farm Lower School

TIGER

Brown as a boxer
But as delicate as glass.
His hearing like a radar
Hunting for its prey.
As fierce as an army
Marching through the jungle.
Eyes like cameras
Looking for its lunch.
Teeth like grinders
Feasting on his catch.

Antony Gray (11)
Newton Road Junior School

GENEVIEVE: THE TIGER CAT

Genevieve is a tiger cat,
She's got huge muscles and no excess fat.
Compared to Genevieve a dog is the size of a mouse
And when Genevieve is tired she'll retire to her house.
Genevieve could take on George Forman
There's not doubt on who would win, for . . .

Genevieve is a tiger cat,
If you are bad she'll hit you with a splat,
And there'll be many a nasty sound
As you end up on the floor
Moaning and very sore.

Genevieve is a tiger cat,
She could make you eat a mat.
Genevieve likes the chair in the corner
For it's near the fireplace where it's warmer.
So if you ever nick her seat
You will be her mince meat.

Genevieve is a tiger cat,
She could run a mile in two minutes flat.
Genevieve is young and wise
People say that she sometimes flies.
Genevieve is tall and is not thin
And she likes a nice big gin.

Genevieve is my cat,
She likes to kill a rat.
Genevieve is nice in a way
She even makes you want to stay.
If you stroke her for too long
She'll rip your hand off
'Cause she's strong.

Genevieve is a tiger cat,
Beware!

Joseph Pepper (10)
Newnham Primary School

SANTA PAWS THE CHRISTMAS CAT

When it's Christmas time for your cat
He'll be waiting on the mat.
There's only one thing on his mind.
Santa Paws the Christmas cat.

He'll be coming down the chimney
Even when it's windy.
He likes mince pies and whisky.
Santa Paws the Christmas cat.

He puts presents in the stockings
Or even on the mat.
He runs as quick as lightning.
Santa Paws the Christmas cat.

Jack Woodcock (9)
Newnham Primary School

CATS

Cats are furry,
Cats are cute,
Cats don't dress
In a suit.

Cats scratch,
Cats bite,
Cats don't fly a kite.

Cats stare,
Cats purr,
And they have fur.

Victoria Gaffney (8)
Long Buckby Junior School

BILLY

My pet rabbit is named Billy
He's sometimes silly.
Jumping and hopping about the place
We very often have a race.
Trying to catch him is very hard
You should see the mess we make in the yard.
He eats the flowers and grass
And plays on the lawn for hours and hours.
When it's time for bed
Where's he hiding?
Under the shed.

Rebecca Bounds (9)
Long Buckby Junior School

PIGS MIGHT FLY!

I once had a dream that pigs could fly
Over the hills high up in the sky.
They soared so gracefully over the trees
Blown along by a gentle breeze.

Everyone in the village came
To see the pigs but all in vain.
All they could see were pink dots in the sky
As they all flew up really high.

One man cried out
"Flying pigs, don't be silly,
By standing out here I'm getting chilly!"

Hannah Gregory (9)
Long Buckby Junior School

CATS

Cats have always got a smile on their face,
If they're happy or they're sad,
But if you are teasing them
They will turn their face down and scratch you.

Stephanie Askew (9)
Kingsthorpe Grove Lower School

AUSTIN THE ODD JOB CAT

Austin is my cat
He is quite fat,
He sits in the sun
'Til there are jobs to be done.
Today before I could blink
He had mended the sink,
That's my sort of cat,
Austin, the odd job cat.

Joanne Trigwell (10)
Newnham Primary School

THE LION

The lion's roar echoes through the dark, gloomy jungle.
He turns his hairy head slowly towards the rocks.
He hears only silent shadows stepping through the trees.
He patrols down to the flowing river.
Raindrops sparkle on his fur.
He knows the enemy is there.
He growls again to give him courage.

BANG!

Sammy Digby (8)
Joanna King (8)
East Hunsbury Lower School

DESERT SNAKE

Dry, slithering across the sandy desert
Searching for a spot for its cool sheltered home
His colours camouflaged in the sand
Yellow, brown and orange
Long tongue springing
In, out, in, out
Searching
Searching
Searching
Melting from the sun
Down
Down
Down
Ahh!
Safe

Sarah Rutter (7)
Belinda Carr (7)
East Hunsbury Lower School

THE FLASH OF SPEED

A female cheetah dashes across the plain
Like camouflaged lightning.

She stops to sniff for danger
She is the fastest thing on earth.

She zooms past so fast
You hardly see her.

Adele Bates (8)
Nicole Melmore (8)
East Hunsbury Lower School

DOLPHIN

He springs up like a frog through the air.
Blue skin shimmering in the sea light
Squealing to his mother
Eyes gleaming like the sun.
Fins flapping up and down on the waves.

Kylie Patterson (7)
East Hunsbury Lower School

SNAPPING VICIOUS JAWS

SNAP! Like a person chopping fish,
Soar through the water silently,
SNAP! Kills another fish,
D
I
V
E
S!
To the bottom of the sea,
Down,
Down,
Down, into the safe sand.

Thomas Mitchell (7)
Lee Ahern (7)
East Hunsbury Lower School

MY NEW PET

My new pet is Jackson the cat.
He is black and white,
He has big green eyes
And a button nose.
I love him lots and lots,
When I go to bed he sleeps on my pillow
Purr purr!

Emma Swords (10)
Denfield Park Junior School

THE POEM

I've got a budgerigar
His name is Sid,
I got him from Pet City
He cost me eight quid,
He's brightly coloured
But mostly green,
The best looking bird
Ever to be seen.

Sam Bland (10)
Denfield Park Junior School

PIGS

Cute,
Smelly oat eaters,
Big flapping ears,
Suck suck, nudge nudge,
Grunt grunt munch munch,
The pigs are all at dinner.
OINK!

Zoe McCormick (9)
Camp Hill Lower School

HORSES

Horses on the farm eating grass
Over the gate galloping fast
Racing flying faster than the wind
Suddenly lightning round the bend
Ever homeward quick as we can
Safe and sound.

Katie Varney (9)
Camp Hill Lower School

PETS

Small rabbits, big rabbits,
Every kind of size.
Fluffy rabbits, spiky rabbits,
With different coloured eyes.
Little fat Guinea pigs with very long hair,
Need good food to eat and tender loving care.
Golden haired hamsters, little fluffy balls,
Like to run and jump about
And also climb their walls.
Budgies like to hop about
And peck food with their beak,
They also like to fly around
Playing hide and seek.
Lots of fish with slimy skin and whippy little tails,
Share their home with family and friends
And not with big fat whales!
Pets are soft and cuddly bringing pleasure to girls and boys,
But remember they are animals
And not just plastic toys!

Samantha Boyle (9)
Camp Hill Lower School

JOSIE

Josie my dog was an Irish Wolfhound
When I needed a pillow she was there lying down,
I put my head on her tummy – soft,
Softer than a pillow.
When my feet were cold
I tucked them under her,
My feet felt like icebergs when I took them away.
Josie – a lovely dog she was,
But now she's gone.
My feet are cold,
And I don't have a pillow.
I get lonely.

Verity Beattie (10)
Broughton Primary School

MY DOG

My dog Marmite died.
I was seven,
He was two.
It was one Friday in July,
I came rushing in from school,
Opened the door . . . nothing,
There he was lying on the floor,
The house felt empty without him,
No barking or scratching.

Hollie Kirk (10)
Broughton Primary School

GRIZZLY BEAR

Grizzly bear is fierce,
He's very, very big.
He wants to catch a seal,
For a very delicious meal.
He shares it with his wife,
They do not have a knife.
Then home they go,
To their cave in the snow.

Patrick Banks (7)
Braunston CE Primary School

THE POLAR BEAR

The polar lands are very cold,
Big polar bears are brave and bold.
No trees or plants in sight,
I see a polar bear having a fight.
A polar bear tries to catch a seal,
For a very delicious meal.
Never warm never green,
All but white and silver sheen.
Mother feeds her cubs on milk,
While she's in the snow like silk.
When spring comes
She'll pop out her head,
While the little ones stay in bed.

Amy Hawkins (7)
Braunston CE Primary School

TADPOLES

Tadpoles have tails.
Tadpoles are in water.
Tadpoles are small.
Tadpoles are slimy.
Tadpoles are black.
Tadpoles look like lollipops.

Sophie Gelsthorpe-Hill (6)
Braunston CE Primary School

COLD

It is cold,
Nothing to grow,
Dark as can be,
Seals barking,
Cubs calling,
Father bear,
Hunter around.

Hayley Goddard (6)
Braunston CE Primary School

TADPOLES

Tadpoles go in the water,
Tadpoles are nice,
Tadpoles eat jelly,
Tadpoles start off being a circle,
Tadpoles turn out a funny shape.

Emily Dyke (5)
Braunston CE Primary School

TADPOLES

Tadpoles look like lollipops
Tadpoles look like suns,
Tadpoles look like fish
Tadpoles look like eggs,
Tadpoles look like faces
Tadpoles look like balls.

Kerran Hanna (6)
Braunston CE Primary School

THE LITTLE FURRY FRIEND

She digs and scratches the newspaper,
Twitches her whiskers.
Her fat, plump body hops around in the cage,
Her mind thinking, who are these people?
She crawls under the straw,
Her ears flip down,
Gurgle gurgle as she sucks
The water from the bottle.

Martyn Drogan (8)
Barby CE Primary School

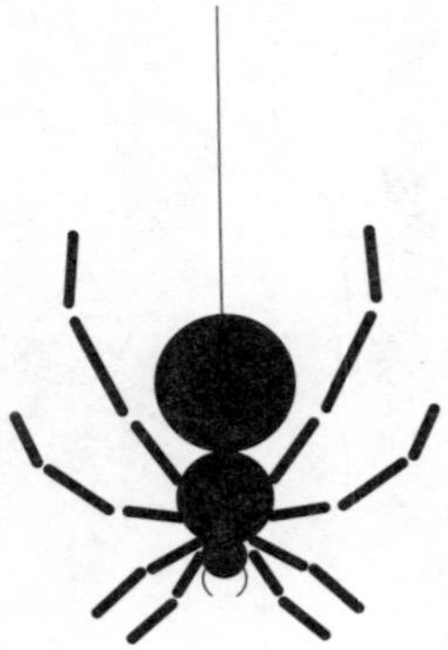

SPIDERS!

Crawling up my arm,
Gazing into my face,
It looked like a round black ball of wool.
Its hairs brushed against me
While it bustled up my arm.
Lightning was going through my head,
The spider came up to my shoulder,
"Take it off!" I yelled.

Ben Roden (9)
Barby CE Primary School

SIMBA THE HAMSTER

The little ball of wool
Plonks his bottom down.
He has an edge of a smile on his face,
He starts to wash himself.
His caramel patches are splodged on him like glue,
He starts to yawn as he snuggles up into a comfy bed.
"Good night,
Or shall I say good day?"

Tamara Lawrence (9)
Barby CE Primary School

THE HAMSTER

The hamster is curled up very
Small it
is asleep
Shhhh! Suddenly
It wakes up
I feel it
WOW! Smooth
Fur so soft
It's like a pillow.

Christopher Horwood (8)
Barby CE Primary School

MY BUNNY

His eye has been forced into the back of his head,
Tail pulled off and chewed by the dog.
Holes in his neck and stuffing creeping out,
His fur has been flattened by lots of loving.
One of his ears is taller than the other,
He lies on my bed waiting for me,
He is a wreck but I still love him.

Ben Roden (9)
Barby CE Primary School

FLUFFY

The loppy eared patchy thing creeps around,
His ears flop and bend like scissors,
The blunt ears are as smooth as his fur,
His eyes slip shut as though he's asleep.
He snatches a bit of his food to eat,
He hits his head on the jail wall,
Puff, he's asleep.

Christopher Osborne (8)
Barby CE Primary School

YELLOW

Yellow is the colour of the blazing sun
Or the colour of pollen that feeds the bees.
Yellow is there on the autumn leaves
You see it again on daffodils bright.
It's there on my pencil,
And when I go wrong,
My bright yellow rubber
Rubs out my mistakes,

Emma Robinson (8)
Whitefriars Junior School

RED

Red is fun,
As fun as jelly,
Sometimes there is
Even red in your belly.
Red is the lovely
Smell of a rose,
I do really hate tomatoes
Red is the look of a fire engine
And a book,
There is a poppy right over there
If you look.
Red is a robin singing in a tree,
I have got a red jumper
Just for me.
I have chips with red tomato sauce,
At home I have got red chalk.
Red is the lovely coat of a fox
And a gleaming tape box.
Red is my favourite colour.

Lauren Addis (9)
Higham Ferrers Junior School

RED

The evil fighting
That brings hate and fear
To all people.
The murder to mankind
In war.
The burned out homes
And towns.
Young children crying
For parents.
The war and anger
That makes death occur
In a sad world.

Clare Borton (11)
Southfield Primary School

COLOURS

Purple makes me happy
Ha ha ha,
Grey makes me sad
Wah wah wah,
Orange makes me hot
Phew phew phew,
Green makes me summery
Lah lah lah,
Brown makes me surprised
Wow wow wow,
Red makes me mad
Grr grr grr.

Natasha Wagstaff (7)
Camp Hill Lower School

BROWN

Brown smells like rotting food,
Brown is mud splashing, slushy,
Smooth chocolate,
Morning coffee, burnt toast,
Caramel slithering down your throat,
Nut brown biscuits,
Brown makes me angry,
Outraged, mad.
People sunburnt on their backs,
Brown reminds me of loud music
Blasting your ear drums.

Emily Longden (10)
Havelock Junior School

GREEN

Green of leaves of grass of trees,
Green of strawberries
Before they're ripe.
A green grasshopper
A frog or a toad,
You may come across one of those.

Saffiya Sheikh (8)
Kingsthorpe Grove Lower School

SILVER

The shimmer of swimming fishes,
As glittery as the silk weaved by the slow worm,
The glisten of the moon,
The twinkle of the stars
And the eye filled with a tear
Glistening in the light.

Karen Lowe (10)
Southfield Primary School

RAINBOW COLOURS

RED IS . . .
Blood oozing out of a cut
Like the colour of a bright red rose,
Tomatoes freezing in the fridge with yellow seeds.

ORANGE IS . . .
Autumn leaves blowing in the wind,
Big round oranges with their juicy fruit
Inside their rough and thick orange peel.

YELLOW IS . . .
A chick all fluffy and fat
Plodding by the yellow haystacks
All large and bushy.

GREEN IS . . .
The grass taking its time
Swaying from side to side,
Juicy fat apples on the tall green tree.

BLUE IS . . .
The still pale water on a light blue pond
And the faint blue sky with blotches of white.

INDIGO IS . . .
The dark blue sky at night
And the dark sea all still and quiet.

VIOLET IS . . .
The colour of pansies growing
And the last colour in the bright rainbow.

Jack Hartwell (8)
South End Junior School

WHITE

My grandad's face
As he lies peacefully in his grave.
A dove as he glides gracefully
Through the morning sky.
The snow as it falls and settles
On the cold, grey ground.
The clouds as they pass on the silent wind.
As my mum shakes the sheets
And they slowly settle on the soft bed.

Gemma Owens (11)
Southfield Primary School

RED RED

A brick is red
Over my head.

Red red rose
Held to my nose.

A ruby is red too.

Blood is red and it comes
Out of you when you get cut.

Sunset is red when the sun goes down.

Anger is red and it shows on your face.

Embarrassment is red
And it makes your cheeks go red.

Robert Williamson (8)
Kingsthorpe Grove Lower School

GREEN

Green, a croaky frog,
The stem of a flower trying to grow,
A slow caterpillar nibbling a lettuce.
Green makes me think of the smell of spring,
Of Fairy Liquid, bubbly and soft.
Of salt and vinegar flavoured crisps
Or of a Granny Smith apple
Sweet and crisp.

Amy Reeve (9)
Whitefriars Junior School

RED

Anger creeping onto faces
On a dark stormy night.
Evil devils frightening people
On the way to hell.
The sign of danger
Before something hazardous happens.
Fires blazing warmly
In small cottages on Christmas Eve.
Blood trickling from injured people
During the wars.

Amanda Dyer
Southfield Primary School

COLOURS

Blue is for my eyes,
Blue is for the sea,
Blue is for the sky
That looks down on me.

Green is for the grass,
Green is for the leaves,
Green is the colour of apples
And of trees.

Black is the colour of the midnight sky,
Black is the colour when people die,
Black is the colour of a witch's cat,
Black is the colour of a velvet hat.

Eleanor Maddison (11)
Long Buckby Junior School

WHAT IS ORANGE?

Orange is a football kit
Waiting to be worn.
Orange is an orange
Or a mango lolly.
Orange flames
Burning bright,
Lightening the darkest night.
Orange is a crayon
The shiniest of the lot.
Or chicken flavoured crisps
Ready to crunch.

Luke Graham (8)
Whitefriars Junior School

WHAT IS RED?

Red is an important colour,
The colour of the sunset
Glowing brightly in the evening.
Red is a spot on your nose,
Or sunburn on your back.
Red is when you get embarrassed,
It is a colour in the rainbow
Or the colour of autumn leaves.
Red is a flower, red rose
Or the colour of danger
What would it be like without red?

James Llewellyn (8)
Whitefriars Junior School

YELLOW

Yellow, yellow
What is yellow?
The sun is yellow,
The lovely shining sun,
It makes you feel warm and cosy,
It shines down on all the plants,
It makes them feel nice.
Yellow means happiness and joy,
I am glad we have the colour yellow,
Are you?

Fiona Wain (7)
Kingsthorpe Grove Lower School

BLACK

As a cloud rolls over a town,
As spirits rise from the dead,
A crow with his cold looking wings
Spread across the stone coloured sky,
The shadows of people
As they walk along the flat pavements
Of the back streets,
An empty feeling deep down inside.

Kim Barber (11)
Southfield Primary School

THE CAKE

We were in the kitchen
Baking a cake
Which we intended to eat with a nice milkshake.
We put in some cherries and *lots* of straw*berries*
But then it started to bubble
And we were in trouble.
It grew and grew,
This fine big brew,
So much we were worried how much we could chew,
It was soon as big as the house
So we got a pin
And stuck it in,
Psssed it hissss*ed*
As it started to deflate,
It landed with a splat on our best china plate,
We were covered in the goo
As it stuck to us like glue,
And the only thing we could do
Was to wash it off in the loo!

Christopher Moreton (10)
Denfield Park Junior School

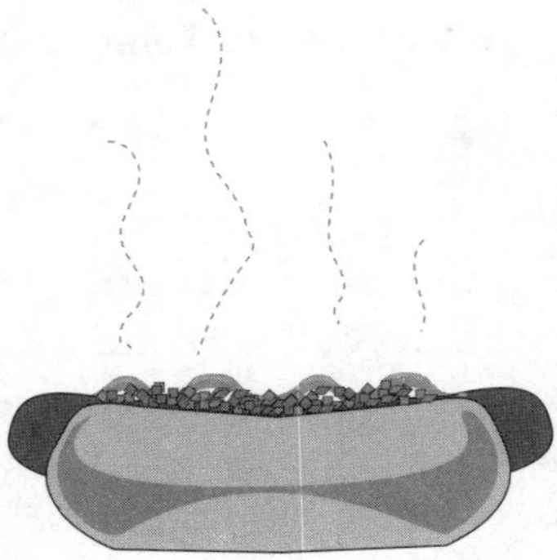

LUNCH

Crunch, crunch goes my lunch,
Hot potatoes and sizzling sausages.
Wobbly jelly for after,
It slithers down my throat
Chocolaty gateaux as well.

Yumm yumm!

Crunch, crunch, goes my lunch.

Gregory Richardson (8)
St Andrew's CE School

LUNCH BOX

In my lunch box I'm sure I'll find
The scrummiest things going round my mind.
Jam tart or an apple pie too
A packet of crisps or a nice warm stew.

I can't wait for the bell to go
And get tucked into my fun food show.
Perhaps frogs legs or pigs nose
I'll eat whatever goes.

The bell has gone I've eaten my lunch
And with a hunch it's back to work.
But I can't wait for dinner tonight.

Joanne Parton (11)
Long Buckby Junior School

CHOCOLATE

Chocolate
Brown, white
Waiting in fridge
I'm going to eat it
Buttons!

Kirsti Jones (8)
Newton Road Junior School

I HATE THAT COFFEE

I like
Milk shake,
I like hot tea,
But I do not like coffee.
I like hot chocolate, I like apples,
But I do not like coffee. I like ice cream,
I like biscuits, But I do not like that
Coffee.

Nicholas Martin (8)
St Andrew's CE Primary School

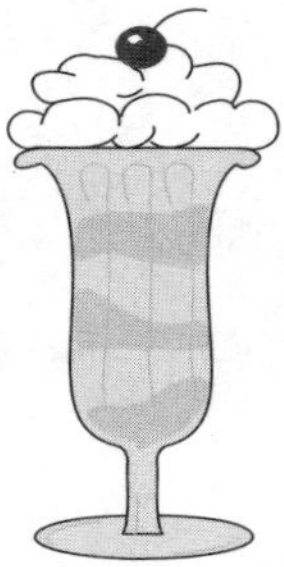

A DOZEN USES FOR APPLES

A refreshing in-between meal snack.
Something to make a delicious pie out of.
Something to turn into a crispy crumble.
An ingredient in a mouthwatering sauce.
A delightful juice drink.
An alcoholic beverage.
A vinegar without malt.
Something to scrump from other peoples gardens.
A target to place on your sons head.
A fruit that is forbidden to be eaten in the garden of Eden.
Something to keep the doctor away.
An interesting topic for a poem.

James Hunter (10)
St Lawrence School

APPLE TREATS

Red apples, green apples,
Brown apples and yellow apples,
Crunchy apples, juicy apples,
Tasty apples and sour apples.

Apples go thump on the ground,
When autumn comes around.
Some hard, some soft and some shiny,
Healthy, fresh and waxy apples.

Apple pie, apple crumble,
Apple turnover and apple puff.
Apple cider, apple sauce,
Apple juice and Appletize.
I like them all.

Jonathan Binley (10)
St Lawrence School

PEAS

I hate peas
The way they run across the floor,
Oh peas please,
Can you not roll any more!
Get back here
And stop trying to escape,
Can't you hear
My fork is stabbing on my plate,
I need you
To finish off my meal,
Can't you do
What would change the way I feel?
On my fork
And away from all that grease,
At last you are caught
So I can eat my meal in peace.

Hazel McNeillie (11)
Long Buckby Junior School

TOAST

A whiff of hot toast
Wafting through the air,
It pops out like a diver
Emerging from the pool.
I pinch it with one finger, one thumb,
Hot!!
I drop it.
It rattles around my plate like a coin.
I slap the butter on.
It melts like snow on a caravan roof.
I twist it and turn it into my mouth.
I glob it down.

Rachel Wilson (8)
Barby CE Primary School

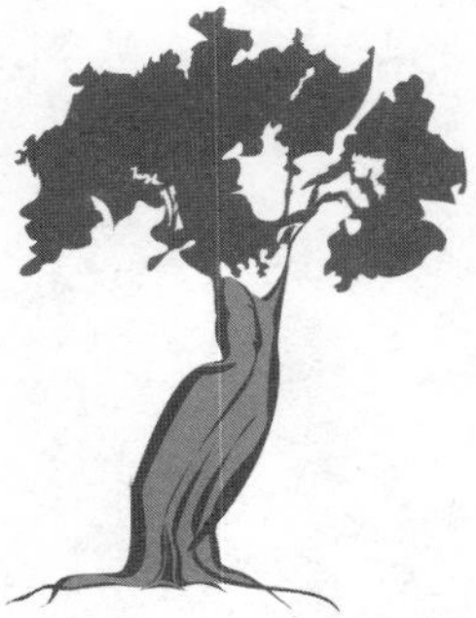

GOODBYE TREE AND THANKS

Goodbye tree and thanks,
I would stay longer
But the wind won't let me stay,
Now the leaf has let go,
It's flying!
I am flying!
He is a golden flyer!
Yes of course he is gold,
Don't you know?
Leaves change colour in autumn.
I am going to catch him,
Missed!

Paul Martin (8)
Whitefriars Junior School

MY TREE

My tree is a spring sort of tree,
It knows when to bud
And it knows when to blossom.
My tree has a big family of animals
Living under its umbrella of leaves,
It's fun to watch the babies born.
Fun to climb
Everytime I come into the garden.
I ask my mum
If she will ever cut it down.
My mum said she will
But I don't think that's true.

Jessica Girling (8)
Grendon CE Primary School

FLOWER POWER

Fragile petals with
Leaves that are soft and moist.
Old scents that are
Weak and hesitant but have no
End.
Rich and graceful petals which are
Soft and smooth like fresh peaches.

Adalina Sacco (10)
Whitefriars Junior School

THE MOON

The moon is a rocky ball floating around in orbit.
It shines like a globe lit up in the dark dusty air.
It floats in space mysteriously.
Every night it changes its phases.
Some nights it is like an apple or a banana.
It shines onto the village down below.
When dawn appears it disappears
Into the big white mountains.
I'll see you in the night
Tomorrow at 7 o'clock outside my house.

Carly Hawkins (11)
Weedon Bec Primary School

TREES

Bright green leaves
On swaying trees,
The sun bursts through the branches.
Some big, some small,
Some short, some tall,
But still I like them all.

Trees to sit under,
Trees to climb,
Trees for happiness,
Trees for life.

Sarah Price (9)
Weedon Bec Primary School

VOLCANOES

As lava goes gushing down
It terrorises the enormous towns.
The beast in the field,
The birds in the sky,
Tremble as the lava sweeps by.
What great energy there is
Look how the mountains spit and fizz.
The rocks and lava are coming near
The red red river that all people fear.

Emma Clark (10)
South End Junior School

HARVEST CINQUAINS

Harvest
Crops gathered
Corn is cut
Ploughing the field.
Field!

Harvest
Rosy apples
Ready to eat
Juicy ripe pears, blackberries.
Delicious!

Harvest
Harvest time
Shops are full
It's freezing out here.
Fields!

Joanna Luck (8)
South End Junior School

THE MOON

The bright glowing moon shines down
Beyond the country, the moon looks like
A velvet sheet dusty and lifeless.

The lonely unhappy moon
Looks like a ghost floating away in space,
Looks like a globe shining in the dark
Turning away on its axis,
Changing it's phase every night,
Like a banana or an orange.

It looks cold and dusky glowing over the city,
Shining like a phantom in the dark,
Slowly disappears away
In the mystery mountains.

Gemma Russell (10)
Weedon Bec Primary School

WATER

My mum says
Water is for washing your face,
Watering plants,
Cleaning the patio
And washing the car.
She thinks it's nice to drink
But I disagree.
I think water is for
Jumping in puddles,
Swimming and having good fun.
So put on your wellies,
Don't watch the telly,
Go out and have some fun.

Tom Hughes (9)
Southfield Primary School

WHIRLPOOL

Water turning round and round,
Water clashing, dashing, bashing,
Waves drown the beach,
Water spinning, flashing, slashing,
Whirlpool sinking ships of all sorts,
Smashing the seas in half and quarters,
White clouds turn into black,
Flashes of lightning lighten the town,
Screaming children fall to the ground,
People dying, children crying,
Sharks and fish fall to their deaths,
Whales swim out of the way,
In the morning children bawling,
The seas start to settle down,

Whirlpool disappears,
Everything becomes normal . . .
'TIL NEXT TIME!

Leon Rawlins (10)
South End Junior School

SPOILT WORLD

The world was once a beautiful place
Which is now spoilt by the human race.

In the rivers people dump pollution
Others have not yet found a solution.

Into the air rises smog
Which is made up of smoke and fog.
In the air the ozone layer is crumbling,
Dangerous suns rays are coming through
And us humans are grumbling.

Into the street the litter flows
Like a river along it blows.
In the streets crisp packets blow
Along with drinks, cans, plastic bags they flow.

In the rivers you see old tyres
With bashed up cars and their wires.

The world was once a beautiful place
Which is now spoilt by the human race.

Emma Baker (10)
South End Junior School

SPOILT WORLD

The world was once a beautiful place
Now it's wrecked by the human race.
And it's time to get rid of pollution
This time there MUST be a solution!
Millions of trees are cut down by the hour
Because the Government don't have enough power.
Newspapers blowing around like mad
Because the people are so bad.
Big black clouds drift into the air
Because factory owners don't really care.
Broken fishing line covered in oil
Strangles wildlife in a deadly coil.

David Green (11)
South End Junior School

SPOILT WORLD

Intense pollution in the air
But still people drive everywhere.
Factories pollute all day long,
As far as they're concerned
They're doing nothing wrong.
Chemicals pour into the ocean blue
It's happening everywhere,
There's nothing we can do.
A suffocating seal in an oil slick,
The people who pollute are really thick.
The streets are filled with paper and litter
If you stop polluting, the world will be fitter.

Joseph Gibson (10)
South End Junior School

WHAT IS THE MOON?

The moon is a circle
With a hole in it.
It is a mirror.
The moon is a hole
In the sky.

Paul Savage (8)
South End Junior School

THE BEAUTIFUL SEA

The seas enriched with dolphins blue,
With golden sand like honey freshly new.
The fish so wonderful, colourful and bright,
A beautiful landscape, a lovely sight.
Sparkling, glittering, dazzling sun,
In the crystal blue water it's so much fun.
The lovely taste of ice cream sundaes,
It keeps you cool on boiling summer Mondays.
The sea is wonderful with its shimmering light,
You can feel the breeze in the dead of night.

Lee Dales (10)
South End Junior School

VOLCANOES

Lava bubbling,
Lava pouring out,
Running down the volcano side,
Burning rock and other things,
Hear the noise of lava,
Suddenly people see the lava in horror,
They run down the hill not noticing
Their homes are burning,
See the black smoke
And hear the crackling of burning trees
And burnt homes,
Smell the ash and volcanic rocks,
The volcano stops and leaves everything black.

Salvatore Santoro (10)
South End Junior School

PLUTO

Damp, wet, freezing cold,
No lifeform, frozen gases,
No heat from sun.

Peter Bedford (9)
Newton Road Junior School

SPOILT WORLD

In the streets you find drink cans,
Paper bags and old hair bands,
In the rivers you find newspapers
Flying out come deadly vapours,
In the air you will find
Deadly smoke and fumes combined,
Now the earth is all polluted
And most rainforests have now been looted,
Animals are now being killed
Deadly liquids are being spilled,
Once the world used to be clean
Until came man and his machine.

James Le Masurier (10)
Duncan Pilling (10)
South End Junior School

SPOILT WORLD

The world was once a wonderful place
But now it's spoilt by the human race.
With nuclear weapons, garbage and tyres,
Trees get chopped down by the hour.

In the rivers, dead fish lay,
Old tin cans where children play.
Tyres, trolleys and plastic bags
Should be banned throughout the land.

Christopher Davies (10)
South End Junior School

EARTHQUAKES

When the room starts to shatter
What is the matter?
Can you see?
What could it be?
It might be an earthquake
Coming for me.
Rumbling, splitting, tearing,
Ripping up the streets,
Crashing, smashing
It's too powerful to stop.

Brendan Murphy (10)
South End Junior School

SPOILT WORLD

In the rivers dead fish lay,
While people laugh about and play.

In the streets people drop litter,
All of this is very bitter.

In the air there's smog and smoke,
It comes from factories with coal and coke.

In the rainforest there's lots of trees,
People chop them down and burn their leaves.

WILL YOU STOP KILLING THE WORLD?

Stacey Mait (10)
Katie Watson (10)
South End Junior School

DAFFODIL

The daffodil sitting there just like the sun,
Just sitting there, just there, having no fun.
Yellow as yellow with different shades you see,
And yellow spring as much as can be.

Its outer petals look like a distant star,
And the leaves go out quite very far.
Its trumpet is like a petticoat, frilly,
Some people call elegant, some others call silly.

What a beautiful soft touch of the daffodil flower,
It always has been soft and never sour.
The petals in the dark beam very bright,
And guide your black way right through the night.

Caroline Fuller (9)
Long Buckby Junior School

FLOWERS

Flowers are seeds at first,
Then they grow a little shoot,
Then the shoot gets bigger
And then bigger and bigger,
To a big flower,
Flowers need lots of water and sun,
You can get different sorts of flowers.

Thomas Walsh (6)
Redwell Infant School

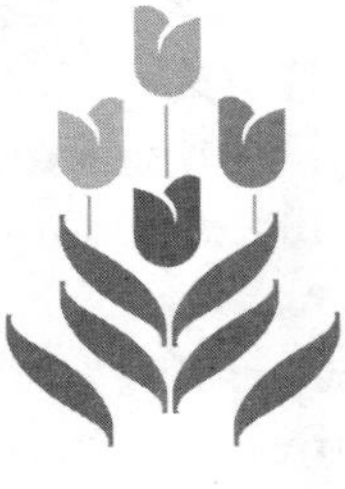

JUPITER

The gases are cold,
Toxic air, so no life form,
A very big spot.

Shelley Ibbotson (8)
Newton Road Junior School

MARS

Small round desert,
Some air, some water, no life,
Dusty, reddish clouds.

Beckey Abbott (8)
Newton Road Junior School

IRIS

One day I was walking through the field,
One lovely day,
Then Iris grew and danced round my feet,
In April coming to May.
When I touched them with my hand
They tickled me round the face,
They were as tall as a door
Twirling round with grace,
They pulled me round in the air
And asked me to dance with them,
They looked so tall and stately
In the lush green field,
Purple and yellow are the colours you know
But I wonder if they ever do show,
The green and white down below,
It would be nice if they did
So we could all admire.

Lauren Addis (9)
Higham Ferrers Junior School

TREE

My tree grows
And
Grows
And
GROWS
With little buds that know
When to come out with a ping!
My tree knows that it's spring!

Kate Barratt (8)
Grendon CE Primary School

MY FLOWER

My flower
Comes out in spring
With all the other flowers.
It stands in the grass
With its friends,
Sparkling in the garden
Under the tree.
It is the only flower
That is red in the green grass.

Jane MacPherson (8)
Grendon CE Primary School

VOLCANO POEM

Steam appearing from the ground
Like smoke from a bonfire.
People scattering like ants
Running from boiling water out of a kettle.

Force building up from the middle of the earth
Smoke starts pouring from the big top,
Shaking from the earth.

A giant tree of smoke above the huge thing,
Ash spraying like confetti,
Evacuation.

People gasping for breath,
Sky as black as the blackest bear in the world.
Boom!

Eruption,
Glowing lava tumbling over itself,
A big sheet of ash covers the land
Like a different world.

Homes spoilt,
People crying,
And mud rivers pouring from the bank.

Carl Wigfield (10)
Havelock Junior School

TREES ARE . . .

Trees are big and trees are small,
Trees are narrow and trees are tall.
Trees are fun for climbing in,
Trees are wide and trees are thin.

Trees are old and trees are young,
Trees are weak and trees are strong.
Trees are blowing in the wind,
Wooden toys should never be binned!

Lianne Norfolk (10)
Long Buckby Junior School

THE VOLCANO

Smoky steam came out from deep deep underground,
From what seemed like a bottomless pit,
Then came the shaking, the ground shook like jelly,
Fiery fury inside, like a furnace sent to destroy,
The jellified earth needed a hot destructive topping,
Suddenly like meteorites from space came down the ash,
Molten ash descended on the city below
Like red hot butterscotch whippy pudding,
Day turned to night,
Ash covered the sky like a thick blanket,
Let no heat out,
It was like a gas oven set to full heat.
The volcano was like the gas,
The source of the heat and the town the oven
Then like a wine bottle being corked.

Matthew Turner (9)
Havelock Junior School

DAFFODILS

Daffodils spread through the fields
With their trumpets high in the air,
Waving their yellow heads about.
Green stalks firmly set in the ground
Swaying in the spring breeze.

Jonathan Partridge (8)
Denfield Park Junior School

SPACE

Star gazing in the night
  What's Orion hunting tonight?
Leo growling,
  Pole star still
Oh! what a wonder,
  Oh! what a sight.
  Shooting stars zooming about,
Too many to count.

Guy Burton (7)
Crick Primary School

ME AND THE SEA

The sea was crashing and banging,
It was dark and misty,
Stones were crashing.
The sea was like a great enormous monster,
Screaming.
The seagulls were calling in terror,
It was cold and spooky,
I was scared.
It was very gloomy,
It looked like knights were all in the sea.

The sea was beautiful and calm,
The clouds were like a woolly pillow,
The sun was like a football on fire,
The sand was dusty and sprinkly and gold.
The sun was sparkling on the sea,
The sea had diamonds sparkling bright.
The blue fluffy sky,
The wiggly sea floating here and there.

Kayte Darbyshire (7)
East Hunsbury Lower School

A WATERFALL ON A SUMMERS DAY

Splashing down like a thud of rain,
Dripping down with a clash at the end.
As it sprays up and splashes back down again,
Glistening in the sun, I see the reflection
Of the sun shining and sparkling on the water,
Shaded by the trees at the bottom.
The clouds cover the sun. It's gloomy and dark.
Very misty and grey as if a waterfall
Is going to pour down on me,
Until the cloud passes on to the east.
The sun is shining again,
A rainbow slightly glows in the distance.

Carrie Peach (11)
Byfield Primary School

THE ENCROACHING TERMINAL

Why in Crick?
It will wipe out all
of the wildlife.
Most animals will
become homeless.
It is DESTRUCTION!

The developers have
no feeling for others.
They are deceitful.

Now everything has been decided.
The dreadful buildings are appearing.
One by one
animals are suffering
and later on
DYING!

It has destroyed the environment.
Pollution, traffic and lots more.

I feel angry and ashamed
because I could not
do anything to stop it.

All we can see now is
buildings dotted everywhere
and the noise of
the trains rushing by.

When Crick thinks back to before
When there were lovely green fields,
rabbits hopping, birds singing
and clean air,
perhaps people will be sorry
they did nothing
to stop it!

Alice Dyer (10)
Crick Primary School

JOURNEY TO HADES

Travelling on the River Styx the water feels cold,
As it swirls the colours wave around the next corner.
The colour looks very cold, blue and black, grey and white,
The sounds of the dead calling to me.
The water dripping from the black ceiling.
I come across a big carving engraved on the wall
Made of stone which gives me shivers down my spine.
I start to play my music, I start to sing.
The soft tender words echo, I turn around corners.
I can see no light just dark, here I am cold and hungry.
The next corner will be Hades.
All I can hear is silence.

Amy Lowe (11)
Byfield Primary School

JUST A TREE

Striding through the gloomy brook,
Looking down the path,
Seeing dark shadows of horses and knights,
I know it must sound daft!

A horses head turns,
It starts to charge,
We start to run,
It looks very large.

The horse turns back.
And starts to run away,
We go forward
The horse is at bay!

We're really close now
I fall to one knee,
I don't believe it
It's just a tree!

Sam Wood (10)
Broughton Primary School

WONDER OF SIGHT WOODLAND PATCH

Every evening I rush to my den,
I lean against a tree,
I look and listen at the wonderful things,
The wren in the hedge singing
Like he's never sang before,
A small brown bird with a plump tail
And see the grey squirrel jumping
From branch to branch with its bushy tail
Bobbing up and down like a wagtail,
The flickering light from the trees,
So much wildlife so much peace,
With the Buzzard soaring overhead like a kite
And the crows screeching in the distance
Like a car with its brakes on.

Christian-Magnus West-Lindell (10)
Byfield Primary School

SUN

Energy-giver
Tan-producer
Seaside-striker
Ice-cream-melter
Leaf-wrinkler
Plant-grower
Body-burner
Puddle-disposer
Day-out-producer
Mud-crumpler
Light-provider
Sweat-sweeper
Puddle-spoiler
Picnic-producer.

Alexander Goss (10)
Whitefriars Junior School

THE WONDERS OF SIGHT

Whoosh! Down the water goes,
All the splendid views,
Torrent of glittering water
Ending silver with white sparkles,
Rich smell of hot sun beaming.

Fascinating thoughts under water,
A big flood has been there,
Leaning over with a long way down,
Lots of spray from the waterfall
Like a cold shower.

Roxanne Peach (11)
Byfield Primary School

MYSELF
An action man
As fearless as a bulldog
Someone dangerous to know
As fast as a leopard
A Cantona extraordinaire
As organised as you can get
A mischief maker
The third Heracles
And excellent drawer.
Cadell Nichol (10)
Boughton Primary School

ME
Nose small
Dark eyebrows
Hobbies art
Tall
Not short
Messy quite
Long hair blond
Grey eyes
TV lover
Age ten
No glasses at all
Memory bad
Not a bit sad
Love animals
Dog, budgie, parrot, hamsters
Lover of chocolate
And cups of tea.
Georgina Mabee (10)
Boughton Primary School

ME
I am active
I am fast
I am gassy
I am jazzy
I am darting
I am cool
I am eager
I am impatient
I am cruel
I am brave
I am bold.
Dean Ainsworth (9)
Boughton Primary School

ME

I am quite big, I think,
I nod and I blink.
I have hazel eyes,
And sometimes I tell lies.
I suck my thumb,
But I am not dumb.
I have brown hair,
And I am not fair.
I have friends, a lot,
When it was my birthday
They never forgot.
Sometimes I get in a stress,
And I make lots of mess.
I like netball,
But I hate to fall.
And I don't like football.
I have a nice personality,
I think,
Sometimes people look at me
And they wink.
I have lots of memories
Of when I was small,
I look rather like a ball.
My behaviour is alright,
Sometimes I get into
A bit of a fight.
Now I have to finish my poem,
Next time watch out about where I'm goin'.

Nina Hayter (11)
Boughton Primary School

MUM

She's got my eyes,
She's got my hair,
Who could it be
Standing there . . .?

MUM!

Natalie Bartosiak (9)
Kingsthorpe Grove Lower School

MY SNOWMAN

On the second of March it snowed all night,
I couldn't believe the beautiful sight.
So crisp, so white, it seemed a shame,
To ruin it in a snowball game.

A snowman seemed a good idea,
So he could stand so tall so near.
A bowler hat would suit his size
And pieces of coal for sparkling eyes.

A nose, oh dear, what can I find?
A carrot is what I had in mind.
Now where's that woolly scarf of mine
I think that that would do just fine.

I went inside to have my tea,
I looked at him, he looked at me.
I hoped he'd still be there next day,
So him and me again could play.

Elizabeth Nichol (9)
Weedon Bec Primary School

SNOWMAN

He shines like a candle
And melts slowly,
He is white and black
And he gets smaller all the time.
When the sun shines
He melts away until another day.

Samantha Dunnett (9)
Southfield Primary School

CLAIRE

Claire is a girl,
Lucky is the name of the pony I ride,
And I feed birds in winter,
I am a happy girl,
Rabbits I like,
Eggs I hate.

Claire Gillman (7)
Newton Road Junior School

MY WORKING MUM

My mum, my mum,
She wants to be a teacher,
She works all day,
She never says a word.

She never takes me horse riding,
She leaves it to dad,
She has to take me to school,
But she needs to work very hard.

She hates the TV on
Because it makes a noise,
She is in the next room,
Studying.

Lucy Mazonas (8)
Southfield Primary School

BEING A CHILD MINDER

Good news!
Sophie has just got a new job
To be a child minder.
Bad news!
How many children is she going to mind?
Forty odd she thinks.
Good news again!
Phew! Only twenty nine children to mind.
Bad news again!
Lost fifteen children, what am I going to do?
Good news!
Found twelve, but where are the other three?
Bad news!
Found the three who went missing.
Oh no!
Twenty went missing, now I've only got nine.
Good news!
Found them all and now I don't think I'll have anymore.

Sophie George (9)
Newton Road Junior School

NURSES

If you want to be a nurse
You'd better like blood and guts,
Because you will see disgusting things
And needle stings.
You will hear screaming from people
Who are hurt badly,
With blood dripping where they are walking,
At the end you will feel sick and grey,
Then you will wait for another day
So you'd better have guts to be a nurse.

Sarah Brown (10)
Newton Road Junior School

PIRATES

They're fierce things pirates,
Waving their daggers about.
They're on a quest to find treasure,
I can tell that without a doubt.

A ship called the Jolly Roger
Set sail in the shining sea,
Sharpening all their weapons
I wouldn't like one to get me.

Thomas Frankland (8)
Lyncrest Lower School

MY MUMMY

I see my mummy cleaning
And guess what I can do?
I use my hands to help
And that's what I will do.
I love my mummy
And she loves me too.

Sian Hopkins (6)
Lyncrest Lower School

A SNOWMAN

Snowmen are very funny,
Noses of carrot,
Out in the cold,
Winter is good for snowmen.
Meg is a snow-woman
Are there snow-women?
No I don't think so.

Thomas Evans (8)
Lumbertubs Lower School

SANTA CLAUS

Late at night when all is dark
Not a single sound is heard,
All the children fast asleep
Except the cat that stirred.

Beyond the clouds
And to my dismay,
The man from Lapland
On his big red sleigh.

I couldn't believe
He had really appeared,
This big podgy man
With a shiny white beard.

He parked his sleigh
On top of the house,
Across to the chimney
As quiet as a mouse.

He take a deep breath
And lays his finger on his nose,
With a big ho ho
Down he goes.

Victoria Mills (10)
Weedon Bec Primary School

MY AUNTY

My aunty calls me a princess,
She's really kind to me,
She helps me with the cooking,
As fast as,
One two three!

Felicity Jacobs (7)
Crick Primary School

MY BROTHER

My brother is nice,
My brother loves me,
My brother is a clumsy boy.

My brother is a funny boy,
My brother is naughty,
My brother is noisy,
My brother is a good boy.

My brother is a silly boy,
My brother drives me potty,
My brother is very good.

Danielle Coghill (6)
Camp Hill Lower School

A VISIT TO CLIPSTON BY THE PRINCESS ROYAL

Princess Anne is coming to Clipston,
Helicopter buzzing like a bee.
We will wave a flag like she's expecting,
Standing, waiting, watching, waving.

I will wear my clean red school jumper,
Princess Anne will open some houses.
And have a cup of tea in the village hall,
Standing, waiting, watching, waving.

Gyles Wilkins (6)
Clipston Primary School

GRANDAD

My grandad is red,
My grandad is funny,
My grandad is kind,
My grandad loves me.

Kerryanne Smith (5)
Camp Hill Lower School

NOISY NEIGHBOURS

I've just moved into the village
And my neighbours are unknown,
I hear them very early
But I'm not about to moan.

Their noise goes on all day
And into the evening too,
I'm almost getting used to it
It's all so very new.

It's like living in a farmyard
I'm really lacking sleep,
You see, the noisy neighbours
Are cockerels, birds and sheep.

Rebecca Rice (11)
Broughton Primary School

MY FAMILY

My dad is nice,
My mum is lovely,
My fish is fun.

My sister is nice,
My sister plays with me,
My mum plays with me.

Taylor Boxall (6)
Camp Hill Lower School

MY SISTER

My sister is clumsy,
My sister is nice,
My sister is naughty,
My sister is a bossy boots.

My sister is clever,
My sister plays with me,
My sister shares,
My sister is funny.

My sister is clumsy,
I like my sister.

Heather Gardiner (5)
Camp Hill Lower School

BROTHERS ARE MACABRE

I feel unhappy when I am sent to my room,
Just because I got mad and went off in a fume.
It wasn't my fault I got in a strap,
It's my brother, he keeps winding me up.
I wish my brother would stop,
He's driving me over the top.
So I lay on my bed and relaxed my head
While I thought of a way to make him drop it,
So . . .
I hit him
And kicked him
And called him names,
You nerd!
You carrot top!
You nit!
And it's working.

Marcus Hamblett (8)
Byfield Primary School

DENTIST

Dentist's drill,
People fainting,
Having fillings,
Moving chair,
Up and down,
In the air,
They all feel ill!

Nicole Evans (8)
Camp Hill Lower School

THE PROBLEM – MY DAD

Tidy your room my dad says,
I hate it when he nags me,
I try to avoid him when he is home,
My dad get angry sometimes,
Eat your dinner,
Don't make waves in the bath.

Jonathan Lautier (9)
Byfield Primary School

MY NAGGING NANNY

My nagging nanny comes round every night
Telling me to get my facts right.
Telling me things I already know
I wish she would buzz off and go!
Every night the same old thing
Nagging and nagging about everything.
Her grey hair sticks to my face like candyfloss
And when she's around she knows who's boss.
Her nose sticks out like a mouldy banana
And when I see her she looks a right 'nana.
Her ears are big and round and red
They really do not suit her head.
Her teeth fell out years ago
And now she's got false teeth to show.

Michelle Chester (10)
Broughton Primary School

MY SISTER

I like my sister,
My sister pulls my hair,
My sister is good.

My sister is rude,
My sister is funny,
My sister is bossy,
My sister likes my mum.

Victoria Stride (5)
Camp Hill Lower School

THE LITTLE BOY

There was a little boy
He hurt his little finger,
He had a little bandage
Wrapped round his little finger.
He went into his little house
And had a little cry,
He had a little sleep.
He woke up
And his little finger was better.

Maisie Maguire (10)
Braybrooke School

MY BROTHER LIAM

Don't you dare ever look at Liam!
Look at his pockets on his coat,
Do you see them?
Inside them pockets of his
Behold some stolen goods
And even my lovely hood,
Guess what he did to his lovely teacher?
When Miss wasn't looking he pinched her bum.
It really hurt – she looked at him in a rage
Like she was gonna' stuff him in a cage.
He screamed and pointed at Ben,
The poor boy began to cry
And then said with a sigh,
"It wasn't me, it really wasn't
Liam doesn't like people,
He really doesn't"
Then Miss turned away,
Guess what?
He did it again.
Miss jumped high into the air
While knocking over her chair,
AND THAT IS LIAM!

Emma Halliday (9)
Barry Lower School

MY BROTHER

My brother is an ant,
He really is quite small,
He scampers about
Getting everywhere,
He's most annoying.

Edward Pryce (7)
Crick Primary School

EDWARD

Edward was a little boy
Wasn't at all shy,
A foe to all of the school
And I can tell you why.

In the morning when he approaches
His pockets are full of cockroaches,
Slugs, spiders,
Ants, snails
And hairy things with slimy tails.

He was expelled from several schools
Because he broke all the rules,
He really is very evil
And his weapons are lethal.

He really is a naughty boy,
When visitors come, he asks,
"Did you bring me a toy?"

This was the last school,
He was expelled at the swimming pool,
The mother asked for another chance
But they replied with a glance.

"Nope! Nope! We cannot cope!
We'll think faster
From this disaster".

Suddenly appeared a spark of luck,
They found a place where Edward could suck
Up all the knowledge of the world,
With a kind and gentle adult.

One day the teacher called him "Buttercup"
His vocabularly measurement went right up,
He stuck his fist into the air
And shouted with a gulp and stare.

"Miss you are a total nerd!"
He shouted loud, everyone heard,
How could Edward be so ruder
To his sweet and beloved tutor?

But one winter when it snowed
His fights went the whole load.
He became a sweeter soul,
Found out by his new friend Noel.

Lance Pursey (8)
Barry Lower School

NETHER HEYFORD

Nether Heyford is good for fishing
Eat from the fish and chip van
The War Memorial is good to remember the war
Harvest Festival at the Baptist Church
Enjoy tea at the school
Ride your bike around the village

Heyford used to have a ford
Every Tuesday the library van comes
Youth Club is on Wednesday
Food store is a good place for sweets
Order your cake from the patisserie
Run around the green
Dance with your friend at the school disco.

Jamie Swingler (8)
Bliss Charity Aided School

NETHER HEYFORD

Newsagent to buy weekly comics
Eat a lolly from the Happy Shopper
Tea from the patisserie
Help at Bliss Charity School
Enjoy a Pantomime at the village hall
Race on the playing field

Have an ice cream from the van
Exercise on the green
You can have fun talking on' phone
Find conkers in Manor Park
Order your medicine from the newsagents
Read books from the school book fair
Dance in the church rooms.

Rebecca Andrews (7)
Bliss Charity Aided School

THE SANDY BEACH

Whooshing, shusshing, curly waves,
Crashing onto the sand.
Crabs pinching me, biting me,
Running after me.
Shells designed, patterned,
Curly, wurly patterns.
Fisher men catching fish, eating,
Being cruel and killing fish.
The pier has wooden floors,
Cracks in the floor.
The sea below my feet.
Birds screeching, squawking,
Swooping down searching for food.
Amusements, bands playing,
People singing, people dancing
Ice cream vans, bells ringing, nursery rhymes,
Buzzing of the fridge.
Seaweed green, sea – smell, fishy smell,
Swimming, diving, jumping, splashing,
Having fun.

Charlene Candler (9)
Vernon Terrace Lower School

IN NORTHAMPTON TOWN

On market day the market comes,
Carrots, cucumber and fruit,
Jumpers, shoes and socks,
It's hot today, I'll buy some pop,
"Eat your fish, get your fish!"
I hear the man shout,
I don't like that smell,
The stalls are selling fast,
I want a few T-shirts for the holiday,
They hang like flopping birds,
I set off home for my tea.

Megan Moss (8)
Staverton CE Primary School

SCHOOL

At playtime the teachers just say this,
NO bubblegum,
NO throwing stones,
Get your coat,
Get your coat,
GET your coat.
I ask to go to the lavatory,
The teacher goes "yes",
I go into the toilets
And there's a big
CROWD.
The water splashing around,
I'm getting all wet,
I hate you,
I hate you,
Please get out of my way.

BANG!

Oh it's too squashed,
I walk out,
People out there shouting . . . People over there fighting,
People angry everywhere,
Boy! I hate playtimes.

Odette Green (10)
Whitefriars Junior School

THE JUNGLE

The macaws fly over the treetops
With other noisy birds down below
On the ground where the tiger prowls around
And the snakes slithering around on the ground
And the giant spiders making webs everywhere
To catch the mosquitoes as they fly by
And the jungle is a creepy place to go.

Stuart Holland (10)
Braybrooke School

THE SEASIDE

I see delicate fragile shells,
The white and blue screeching birds
And the green floppy seaweed.
I see the yellow and brown beach,
I hear the roaring, splashing sea,
And the loud band playing.
I hear people shouting and speaking,
I hear music on the ice cream van.
I smell vinegar on fish and chips,
I can smell the sweet thrusting sea,
I can smell the salty air.
I built the tall, breaking sandcastles.
I play games on the beach
And collect the delicate, smooth
Fragile curly shells.

Ursula Naji (8)
Vernon Terrace Lower School

BIRMINGHAM 1869

This growing city
With its increasing suffering,
Agony and distress,
Children crying.

A young boy,
His clothes in tatters,
Stands watching the gloomy scene,
He can see the wasted landscape.

The sun,
Hidden by black clouds,
Cold, unfeeling,
Darkness covers the city,
Factories spew out
Smoke to add to the smog.

Filthy, dull and
Polluted city,
People heave sighs
As the day ends.

Ellie Skinner (11)
Southfield Primary School

THE BAPTIST CHAPEL

A simple wooden cross
Above the pulpit hangs
On the tall strong wall
That surrounds the chapel.

A deep blue pit,
The baptistery
Where many a Christian is immersed.
Gaping wide open like
A hungry bird waiting
To be fed.

The balcony,
With its musty smell,
Elaborate decorations,
Stands out from the rest
Of the plain building.

But however plain and simple
It is a holy place
To worship God and Jesus
And is appreciated by all.

Ruth Underwood (10)
Helmdon Primary School

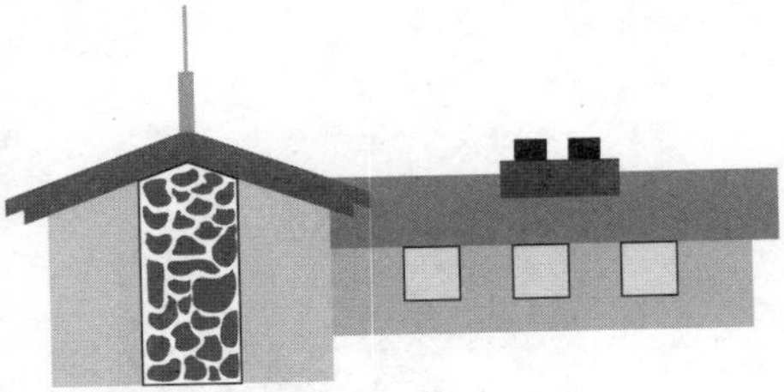

SCHOOL

I like Friday
Get away from topics,
No more forces
No more Odette.

I hate Mondays
Coming back to school,
Teacher yelling
Underline your date.

Tuesday is worse
Games time,
Oh no
Every one runs in the hall.

I like Friday best
So I can retire
For the weekend
And just relax.

Claire Morris (9)
Whitefriars Junior School

IN THE PLAYGROUND

I was doing what I did best,
Running
With my friends,
My best friend stopped.
"You can't play" he said.
An argument started,
He called me a name,
"BR-R-EWSTER!"

My dogs name!
I hit him,
He fell over,
Got up and ran away,
I was embarrassed.
Everyone's looking!
Annoyed,
Why did he say that?
Sad,
I've lost my friend . . .

Bruce Goodridge (11)
St Lawrence School

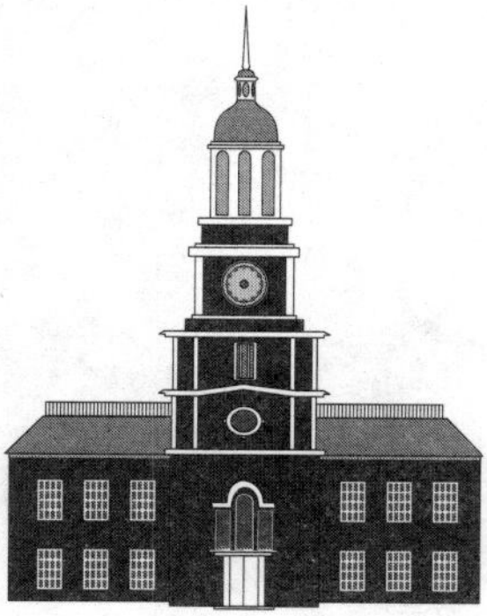

VICTORIAN CITY

Looking down
On a Victorian city,
All I see is
Grey, brown, red.
The air is smoky
And I hear children
Crying in the streets.

It is early
In the morning
And people,
Weary, sad,
Go to work in the factories,
All day they work
In appalling
Conditions.

The gloomy, dull city
Is cold, dark,
The black smoke
Towers up into the sky,
People die from diseases
They have caught from the polluted air.

Jayne Harris (11)
Southfield Primary School

THE COCA COLA WAREHOUSES

The warehouse is big
And extremely tall,
You hear the lorries all day long.
The workmen are happy
At the end of the day,
They are glad that their job is done.
At the end of the week it's wages time,
Some are happy with what they've got,
Some are told to work a bit harder
And only get a few pounds and are told
"That's the lot for this week!"
Home they go to bed,
It's been a hard shift.

Amanda Shaw (7)
Staverton CE Primary School

AT THE SEA SIDE

The sand,
The seagulls
And the tide coming in
Are all very well,
But the best thing is
Sandcastles
And sitting in the sun.
But then it comes,
The tide is in,
And it washes your things away.

Christopher Frost (9)
Lyncrest Lower School

THE FAIR

I went on a roller coaster
It was very scary,
I came off pale white
Then I fell on the floor.

I went on a ghost train
It was very scary,
I came off pale white
Then I fell on the floor.

I went on the water slide
To cool me down,
I came off freezing cold
And I had to dry myself off.

Joanna Serbyn (7)
Kingsthorpe Grove Lower School

OUR SCHOOL

Our school is a hundred years old,
We have a bell tower on top of our school,
It is in the middle of town
With a bird table in the playground,
We are next door to the infant school,
The dining room is across the playground
And the outside toilets are there,
We like our school.

Stacey Hemmington (7)
Claire Gillman (7)
James McKenna (7)
Mark Bailey (7)
Newton Road Junior School

HELMDON

Houses in streets
Eager faces
Loving faces
Music
Daring places
Old viaduct
No ordinary village.

William Gidman (9)
Helmdon Primary School

ALL SAINTS CHURCH

A grand figure of All Saints Church
Stands in all its splendour.
Inside the protective, stone sculptured walls
Lies a spacious place of worship,
With decorous structures covered with intricate patterns
Of angels, archangels and all the company of heaven,
Fringed with gold.
The gleaming woodwork is marvellous,
Luxury surrounds you as you stand before the altar.
Exquisite and picturesque
In the peaceful and evermore holy place
Of All Saints Church.

Ruth Underwood (10)
Helmdon Primary School

100 YEARS OLD TODAY

It's my birthday,
100 years old today,
I have red bricks
Just like burning flames
Surrounding me.
My bell tower still stands,
It's cold, damp and spooky inside.
My lead roof
Is growing green hair.
My playground aches
As the children hurry in
At 8.50, then
Do the same at twenty past three,
Then, finally then,
I can lock myself up,
Snuggle down
And have a good night's nap.

Rebecca Ekins (10)
Newton Road Junior School

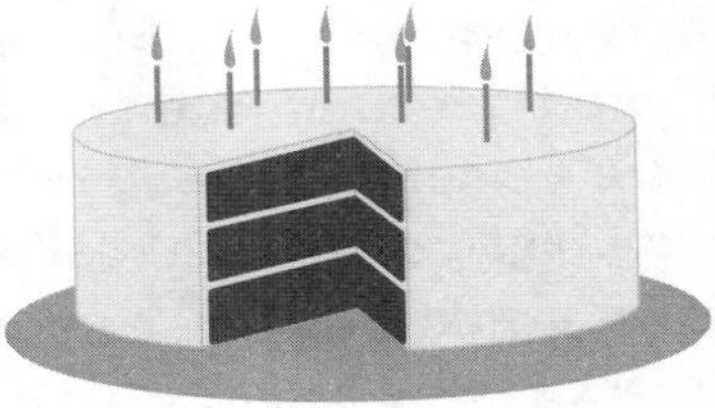

HAPPY BIRTHDAY SCHOOL!

People teach you,
Children play,
Classroom, playground, everyday.
In the library children read,
Teachers watch for every need.

Classrooms warm, never hot!
Must put glue in the pot.
Pictures hanging on the wall,
Sometimes big, sometimes small.

Bell rings at half past three,
Going home now, time for tea.
Mum's waiting at the door,
Children running by the score.

Christopher Bergin (10)
Newton Road Junior School

GROWING UP IN NORTHAMPTON

Northampton is the place to be,
There's lots of things to do and see.
It's one great adventure when you're a child
But when you get older you'll still like the style.
So come on down to see McDonalds, Toys 'R' Us
And Abington Park.
There's Salcey Forest and Wickstead Park
Where I'd recommend you'd better start.
There's cinemas where I go to have a laugh
And Lings Forum with really great staff.
Roller skating's great, so are gymnastics,
Bezerk's good to have a good play about,
So at the end of the day I'm sure you'll surely sing
Northampton is where I'd rather stay.

Kanda Rogers (8)
Cedar Road Lower School

GROWING UP IN NORTHAMPTON

I like Northampton because of the week,
Mondays I go to town,
On Tuesday I go to take the library books back,
On Wednesday I go swimming,
And on Thursday I go back to town,
On Friday I go to my friend's house,
On Saturday my friends take me to Plaza,
And on Sunday they take me to Bezerk.

Lucy Davies (9)
Cedar Road Lower School

HELMDON

Homes and houses
Exciting days
Lessons in schools
Mummys pushing prams
Daddys doing work
Old people walking in the streets
Nannys looking after children.

Rosie Llewellyn (7)
Helmdon Primary School

THE RAIL FREIGHT TERMINAL

Everything is peaceful,
Nobody around,
Then suddenly destructive machines
Come into the scene.
They start tearing up the land,
Crops lying there dead.
Terrified animals hurry away,
The air turns foul and polluted,
Angry people come in shouting,
"Why our village,
Why Crick?"
The loss of countryside brings great sorrow.

Nicholas Young (10)
Crick Primary School

NANNY'S HOUSE

Nanny's house is
Cosy and comfortable,
Warm and welcoming,
Tiny and tidy,
Full of things,
Flowers and photographs,
Cushions and clocks,
Tea pots and trays,
Bread and butter,
Doors and doorbells,
Grandma loves me.

Richard Lawson (8)
Crick Primary School

HELMDON

Helpful laughing children
Enjoyable singing in the church
Living in cosy homes
Mothers and fathers
Dogs barking in the garden
Old people walking in the street
Naughty people like my sister.

Sarah Quiney (8)
Helmdon Primary School

THE UNIVERSE

The Universe is a sea of black
Containing wonders beyond belief.
Take, for example, stars, shooting stars,
The Concordes of the sky,
Leaving jets of light wherever they fly.
Galaxies, trees in a forest,
A forest called the Universe,
Or planets, children of the Universe,
Basis of life where discovery never ends.

I look up from Earth and I see
Stars twinkling in a sheet of black velvet.
Children wonder as they stare up at a moving light
They think is is a shooting star.
Mouth wide open, eyes staring,
Waiting for a magical moon to come out.

Rob Hall (10)
Byfield Primary School

THE STREET

Cars beeping,
BEEP BEEP!
Children playing,
What a racket.
Mothers talking,
YEAH YEAH!
Babies crying,
WA WA!
People shouting out of cars,
MOVE MOVE!
Here comes the rain,
PITTER PATTER!
Mum says,
"COME IN COME IN!"
Rain stops,
START AGAIN!

Francesca McLafferty (9)
Crick Primary School

SCHOOL

School is where I learn
Children play together
Here is my classroom
Our school is fun
Off we go out to play
Lyncrest is the best.

Steven Cotton (6)
Lyncrest Lower School

CASTLE ASHBY

Castle Ashby's a beautiful place
But you don't meet the Marquis face to face.
Look in the pond for toads and newts
Hide in the hedges, look for roots.
The geese squawk so terribly they dance
A little jig for me and family.

Hannah Brown (8)
Cedar Road Lower School

MY TREE HOUSE

When I am in my tree house
It is as if I can see the whole world.
Fields are all around me
With the sun shining like butter melting.
You can see all the houses down my street, like stairs.
You can see people talking over fences
With the dogs laying down not bothered what happens.
The gardens look like garden shops as the ponds glitter.
The tree flows side to side like waves,
So peaceful so quiet in my little place.
Troubles just drift away,
So many bright wonderful things to see
In my magic world.

Gemma Beech (11)
Byfield Primary School

ST. BENEDICT'S

Warm and comfortable
Is St Benedict's,
Tall and peaceful
Reaching to God.
Filled with joy and full of interest
Prayers are said in a quiet surrounding.
Bells shall ring for great celebrations,
Warm and comfortable is St. Benedict's.

Julian Breen (9)
East Hunsbury Lower School

THE HOUSE DOWN OUR STREET

The house down our street
Has curtains that always meet.
No one comes out
Even when there's no one about.

No one knows who lives there
To knock on the door,
Who would dare?

Now I'll end my poem with this.
I would never go in the house down our street
With curtains that always always meet,
Because it's eerie, dark and scary
And it makes us very wary.

So it you're of a curious nature
And you are in Broughton one day,
Come along and see the house but
I won't come, NO WAY!

Elizabeth Leaver (11)
Broughton Primary School

WAY UP IN THE MOUNTAINS

Way up in the mountains I can see
A lot of things but mostly trees.

Way up in the mountains I can hear
A song thrush's song loud and clear.

Way up in the mountains I can smell
Fresh summer breezes and flowers quite well.

Way up in the mountains I can feel
Soft green grass, a goat's favourite meal.

That was a long time ago
That was before the lumberjacks came,
The trees are no more.

Way up in the mountains people will frown
For all that is there is a dumping ground.

Owen Hammond (10)
Broughton Primary School

THE CROCODILE FIELD

A special place
That's dear to me,
Is not a church
Or an old oak tree.

A field where I like to walk
When the weather is hot and the sky is blue,
With my mum and dad
And my sister too.

Imaginary crocodiles
Chasing me,
Through a field of crops
Like an endless sea.

It's not a church
Or an old oak tree,
A field
Very dear to me.

Jodie Holland (11)
Broughton Primary School

THE BLACK DOOR . . .

I used to know a nasty door
Near the hospital, was it number 4?
It had tons of eerie, peering eyes,
No, I'm not telling lies!

The eyes glittered shining gold,
They never grew tired, they never grew old,
They always followed our nice clean car,
Then I wished that we were far.

Away from this horrid gleaming door
But where it used to be before . . .
There stands an ordinary wooden door
And now it's safe, I'm really sure!

Natalie Burton (10)
Broughton Primary School

THE WHOLE YEAR THROUGH

Christmas is over
And January breaks
The cold grey skies of December.
Looking at them will
Make you think and
Surely let you remember
The
Long
Hot
Days
Of summertime
And the chilly
Autumn days too.

So . . .
When the spring buds open
We can see
The whole year through.

Ruth Humphreys (9)
Kingsthorpe Grove Lower School

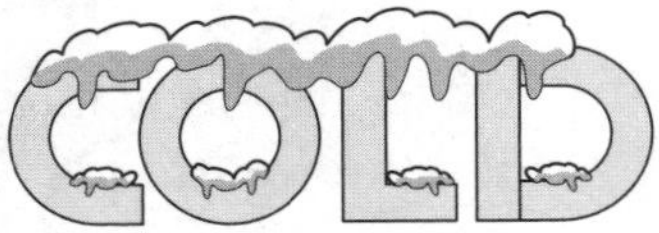

WINTER YOU'RE SPECIAL IN A WAY!

When I open my eyes in the morning
Still all I see is black.
I tear the curtains open
As the sun barely comes up.
I see the winter,
Then slowly, I talk
And I say:
"Winter I love it when you scatter your frost
Around me like a coat to comfort me.
Now I know why you are so special.
With the enchantment of the mist like angels singing,
Tell me winter when will you show everybody
What you really are like?"

Victoria Pritchard (10)
Newton Road Junior School

DECEMBER

The trees in December have bare branches,
They sound as if they are whispering
Creepy words and howling like dogs.
The leaves twisting and twirling,
Brown, yellow and gold.
They are crunchy and crackly if you step on them.

When I walk home from school at night
It's quite dark, it's cold and my fingers tingle.
They feel like ice cubes.
When I get home I warm myself by the fire.
I feel cosy in my house,
Safe from the dark and cold night.

The weather in December is a wind howling
Against the windows trying to push itself in.
The rain falls down,
making little splashing sounds in the puddles.
The dew on the grass looks like diamonds
That have fallen from the sky.
It's frosty, cold and misty outside.

Rebecca Anderson (10)
Byfield Primary School

WINTER

A roaring sound as the wind gusts,
Wet as a tap dribbling,
The frost catches our nose.
Icicles dropping,
Smashing as they fall.
Children playing with rosy red cheeks.
As the wind stops,
Soundless fog goes on and on for miles.
As the ice settles,
It's as slippy as our kitchen floor.
Winter!

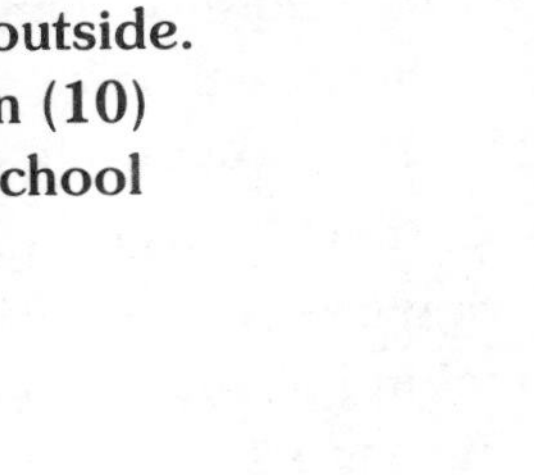

Hayley Buttery (11)
Newton Road Junior School

AUTUMN

The wind whistles like a boiling kettle,
The leaves fall like cornflakes into a bowl,
They crunch like crisps in a small bag,
The mist comes down like a white fresh blanket.
The car exhausts are like steaming hot baths,
The birds fly away like a swarm of bees,
The evenings get dark as the night draws in,
Our home is like a cosy bear cave.

Kelly Evans (10)
South End Junior School

WHITE SPRING

The delicate bird foot prints wandered around aimlessly,
I could just make out the little robins,
Their red breasts glimmering against the pure white snow.
Suddenly the white flakes of snow tumbled down,
All I could see was white.

At last the sparkling snowfall started to disappear.
The thicket of evergreen was drooping
With the weight of the snow huddled in lumps.
In a tight corner were small thin trees,
These were covered in sleek iced snow.

I walked away from the trees
Hearing the crisp snow,
Crunching as my feet went deeper into the white blanket.
As I turned around I saw the frozen water of a pond,
Its glassy surface looking up at me.
What was it trying to say?

Again the crystals of white started to fall.
I turned away but I still saw white.
As I looked to the floor my shadow appeared,
It was pure black.
The glare of the sun warmed my tingling fingers
As the snow began to melt away.

Alexandra Eastham (10)
Weedon Bec Primary School

AUTUMN DAYS

Autumn days when the grass is jewelled
and the conkers in a chestnut shell.

Usually patchy fog and damp earth
and shorter days and longer nights.

Twirling golden leaves spinning to the ground.

Until suddenly a mist of fog covers the trees
and then it goes and you can see all the leaves again.

Most of the grass is glittery
and apples are falling from the trees.

Nuts are being collected by the squirrels
and other animals.

Daily they fall such wonderful colours
and beautiful shapes and patterns.

Away they go to give their tree a rest.

You can see the bare trees
where all the leaves have left and fallen.

Still, winter's on its way!

Samantha Tilley (9)
South End Junior School

IN AUTUMN

The wind whistles like a teacher
Blowing a whistle for the end of playtime.
The leaves fall like corn from the back of a harvester
And crunch like paper tearing.
The mist comes down like clouds falling from the sky.
Car exhausts are like smoke from a chimney.
Birds fly away like feathers getting blown away in the wind.
The evenings are like black paint all over the world.
Our homes are like electric blankets.

Sally Hunt (10)
South End Junior School

SUMMER SUN

In the summer
My body is like a boiler.
I feel like I've just been sizzled
In a hot frying pan
Full of my omelette.
It's so hot it feels like the sun
Is melting on my head.
In summer the golden sun
Sticks out his flaming hot tongue
And touches me to say it is morning.

Rosie Capewell (8)
Whitefriars Junior School

SPRING

In the spring
The birds sing.
There are lots of flowers
And April showers.
The sun shines brighter
The days are lighter.
We play in the sun
And have lots of fun.

Zara Hudson (10)
St Lawrence School

SPRING

Spring is such a happy time,
Everybody is having fun
And enjoying the sun.
We have April showers
To help the flowers.
New animals are born
The fields are full of corn.
The mornings are brighter
The nights are lighter.

Lynette Maclean (10)
St Lawrence School

AN AUTUMN DANCE

The colours of leaves that are falling, falling
The world is a mass of rich colour.
Sweet chestnuts shed their prickly shells.
Leaves performing a special dance
For Mother Autumn to share.
An early morning frost graces the ground,
Brother Wind blows a swift blast all around.
An early darkness falls and all is silver in the moonlight.
All is still, everything and everyone is asleep.

Anna Rylance-Murdoch (10)
Pitsford Primary School

SPRING

Spring time is a happy time,
Primulas unfurl their petals,
Rabbits racing in the fields,
In the meadows lambs are bleating,
New life fills the land,
Glorious days with lovely sunshine.

Eamonn Morrison (7)
St Brendan's Infant School

A SPRING POEM

Spring sunshine shining on me
Pretty petals growing back
Rushing rabbits through the grass
Insects crawling all about
New baby animals being born
Grass growing tall.

Stephanie Nelson (7)
St Brendan's Infant School

SPRING

Spring is a start of a new year
Primroses grow in flower beds
Red nose day comes again
In spring Lent comes
Now it is getting warm
Green grass is growing.

David Haughton (7)
St Brendan's Infant School

HAIKU

Spring is in April,
Spring is sunny and windy,
Flowers start to grow.

Stacey Hemmington (7)
Newton Road Junior School

WINTER

Wind blowing hard
Ice with water underneath
No one about all snuggled inside
Tears running down your eyes
Ears hear the rain outside
Rain dripping off the roof tops.

Stephanie Nelson (7)
St Brendan's Infant School

WINTER WAYS

Winter has approached,
A blizzard of snow clothes the ground
With water and ice all around.
We put on our coats and gloves to keep warm,
Step outside there's a monstrous storm.
Slipping all the way down the street,
Quickly get in it's starting to sleet.
Then it seems that spring is late,
Now all I can do is wait wait wait wait!

Lee Newell (11)
Newton Road Junior School

SUMMER

It's hot in my garden
I'm sweating all day,
Seas are glittering bronze and gold
Whilst I play.
It feels like I'm in a deep fat fryer,
Barbecues burning all day long,
Flowers weeping,
There's too much heat.
I hear the ice cream van
But there it goes.
Mum is soaking me in suntan cream,
I wish winter would come.

Grant Cooper (9)
Whitefriars Junior School

AUTUMN

Autumn is not my favourite season,
Umbrellas don't go up,
Trees leaves are going to colour,
Usually leaves go to the ground,
Mums tuck you in warm beds,
Nests are not with us.

Autumn great,
Autumn colourful,
The leaves dropped to the ground,
And feet on leaves CRUNCH!
Autumn is not my favourite season.

Amy Pinner (10)
South End Junior School

WINTER

Winter is cold,
It isn't hot.
It snows, it rains.
I like winter
Because the snow is cold,
It isn't hot.
In the winter it is Christmas
And you get lots of presents.

Lisa Allen (7)
Lyncrest Lower School

SPRING

Sun is shining on the flowers,
Plants are lovely,
Rabbits go running in spring,
Insects are crawling in spring,
Now leaves are turning green,
Great isn't it to see spring!

Lauren Fowkes (7)
Lyncrest Lower School

THE WINTERY DAY

Outside it is cold and icy,
White diamonds on the ground,
The sky is misty and wet,
Trees are frozen,
Hands go numb,
People leave footprints in the snow,
The day goes on,
The sky gets clear,
Frost is melting,
Night gets near.

Inge Verwoerd (11)
Long Buckby Junior School

WINTER

Some people like winter
When the snow falls
On the paths, trees
And on the walls.

My dad doesn't like winter
When the snow falls
On the paths, trees
And on the walls.

Laura Gibson (8)
Lyncrest Lower School

WINTER SNOW

The snow floats softly gently onto the road
Stopping traffic of all sorts,
People are shovelling snow from the frozen roads.
I see snow from out of my window like a giant blanket,
The children go out wrapped up warm
Children throw snowballs and make funny snowmen.
Trudge, trudge, I trudge through the snow.
The trees are covered with sparkling snow and look ghostly.
The ponds are frozen and the ducks scrabble on the surface.

Sarah Galletly (9)
Chipping Warden Primary School

AUTUMN COLOURS

Brown is the soil where a brown rabbit burrows
Across the land in a field full of furrows.
Brown are the leaves that fall from the trees
And down, spinning round and round,
Come the seeds of the sycamore tree.
Now it's late and getting dark,
Brown for the squirrel asleep in her dray
And brown for the horse asleep in the hay.

Red is the sun as it sinks behind the hill
And red is the wall of the old windmill.
Red is for the fox prowling through the farm
And for the apples stored in the barn.
Red is for the berries on a tree by the stream
And red is for the farm house where the children dream.

Silver is the moon sailing high in the sky
And through its glow the barn owls fly.
The silver stars cast their light
And moths fly around hidden from sight.
The grey clouds hide the moon
And everything is still.

Hannah Gregory (9)
Long Buckby Junior School

SPRING

Spring is a man who leaps about
Calling for the flowers to come out.
Making the sun bigger and brighter
Coaxing the moon to shine that little bit whiter.
Helping the blossoms come out on the trees
Giving some freshness for the breeze.

Helping all the plants to grow
And melting all the ice and snow.
So when the children wake up the next day
They can all go out to play.

Amy Cull (10)
Higham Ferrers Junior School

FALL

Goodbye summer,
Hello autumn,
Red, yellow, brown,
Golden the leaves
And soon they will be saying
"Fall!"

Natalie Bartosiak (9)
Kingsthorpe Grove Lower School

AUTUMN IS . . .

Misty mornings with magic shining sun,
Dew on the grass like diamonds,
Rosy ripe apples just juicy for me,
Leaves falling from the tree,
Red and gold rustling leaves,
Crunching on the ground,
Animals curling up in balls
Ready for hibernating,
Dark cold cosy evenings
I'm ready to go to bed.

Erika Merson (8)
East Hunsbury Lower School

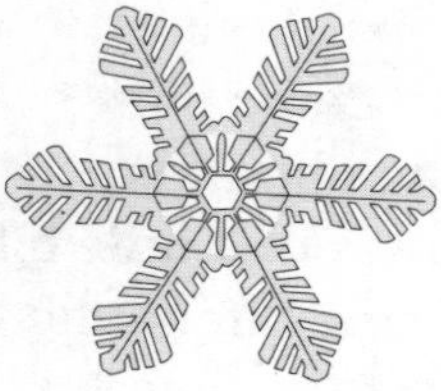

SPRING

Sticky buds and
Pussy Willow in the woods.
Rabbits scampering
In the fields.
Nest building birds
Getting twigs.

Jamie Hextall (7)
Crick Primary School

WINTER SNOW

Icicles form like glittering glass
Frozen on cottage roofs,
They melt one by one
When the icy wind knocks them.
Hail and sleet clatter to earth
Hitting everything with tremendous force
And shaping the soft crispy snow into fantasy figures.
Further snow slowly settles on the earth,
Forming a silky coat of white,
Spoilt by crisp footprints here and there
Which slowly melts away into the night.

Hannah Stagg (10)
Chipping Warden Primary School

AUTUMN DAYS

Air moist, fresh and clean.
Unnoticed smells of manure drifting.
The stream is clear, gurgling, shining.
Umbrellas ready? It's wet and damp.
My feelings are happy and settled.
Nobody sees the grass, soft springy cool green.

Don't you notice the trees drifting spiralling leaves?
And the smell of wet leaves.
You don't see the sky, pale blue, white.
Sounds of birds singing, rustling leaves.

Lisa Walden (9)
Byfield Primary School

WINTER SNOW

Skiddy ice and frosty snow
Become slippery and crispy,
The snow falls from the cold grey sky,
The transparent icicles
Hang from the wintry ghostly trees,
Look closely, look closely,
See the weird shapes the snow makes,
The winter flakes are cold and wild.
The blanket of frost drifts down the aisles of trees,
Each star is newly forgotten,
As faces are lost in their own shapes.

Lia Jones (11)
Chipping Warden Primary School

WINTER SNOW

Today the snow is floating down.
The children have snow on their heads,
It is like a crown.
They break icicles
For the snowman's nose.
On the grass the snow is really deep.
I stay inside because it is too cold.
Children are happy but so am I
Because I went out before them.

Jason Hopkins (8)
Chipping Warden Primary School

WINTER SNOW

Today the snow is very deep.
The snow is floating down.
The snow covers houses
And it shines in the sun.
The snow covers the trees
And the wind blows it into patterns.
Children play in the snow.
The snow covers cars.
Children play snowball fights.

Luke McNeill (8)
Chipping Warden Primary School

AUTUMN

A nice breeze through the air
  blows the trees around.

Up above, clouds in the sky,
  they are always floating by.

Two old people walking through the leaves,

Under the leaves there are different colours,

Miserable weather is around the corner,

Noises in the background,

Down come the leaves from the trees
  that means autumn is coming,

Autumn is nice and fresh

You think the stream is glass.

Kevin Moyce (10)
Byfield Primary School

WINTER SNOW

The winter snow falls slowly softly to the ground.
People are running on the soft crispy white snow,
Snowy road.
Children play in the street throwing snowballs
And making footprints in the snow.
In the morning I stand out of my door
Seeing the snow gently falling down on the drive.
Watching glittering snow fall on the ground
And snowmen melting on the grass.
Fields roads and pathways are filled with snow
Melting quickly after a day.
The trees are covered with glittering white ghostly icicles.

Juliet Molloy (9)
Chipping Warden Primary School

SPRING

Daffodils swaying in the breeze
While buds appear on the empty trees,
Lambs are hopping and skipping around
And flowers appear down on the ground.

The sun shines brightly up in the sky
While singing birds fly up high,
At last the spring's here
And winter has gone for another year.

Hannah Gregory (9)
Long Buckby Junior School

AUTUMN TIME

A dazzling beam of light on the grass,
Unusual leaves fluttering from the sky,
Trees bare. A carpet of leaves on the ground,
Up above the trees a mist is forming,
Mums are hurriedly fetching washing indoors,
No hustle and bustle, just laze about,
Dads planting bulbs to flower in the spring,
And people stay indoors more if they can.
You love autumn with its lovely colours and splendour.

Lisa Walden (9)
Byfield Primary School

WINTER SNOW

Slowly the soft white snow falls from the sky
Melting as it floats to the ground.
The fields are camouflaged in a white blanket,
Glittering icicles cling to window sills.
White star-like flakes of snow float through the sky
And gently hit the floor and die.
Wrapped up warm in the brittle snow
Trees look beautiful dressed in their white coats,
While houses look like ghostly figures
Huddled silent side by side in the winter snow.

Karra Banks (9)
Chipping Warden Primary School

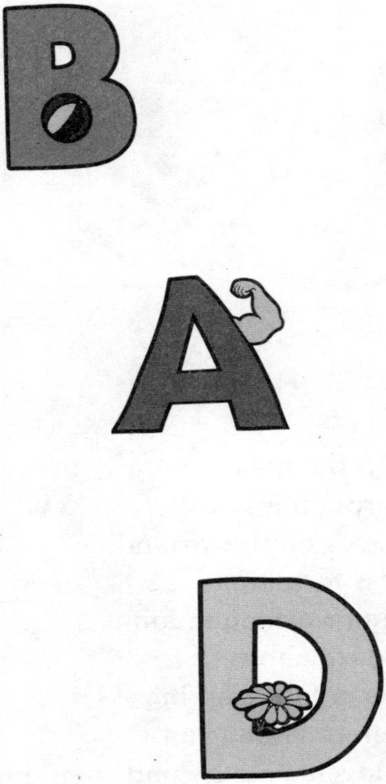

IN 1995

In 1995
Boy! Is the world bad.
All that fighting and tension.
How can I help?
How can little me help
When it's all so bad?
Everyone else is wrecking my world.
Why should I care?
But I do.
I can forgive if I can.
That should help.
I can decide not to join in,
Not to hurt others,
Not to fight,
Not to drink,
Not to smoke,
Not to take drugs,
Not to pollute,
To make the world a better place.
If enough of us
Do the same,
Boy! WHAT A WORLD!

Jim Ormond (11)
Culworth CE Primary School

ANGER

Anger is red like the planet Mars,
Anger tastes like vinegar
With its sour acidy fizzle.

Anger smells like burnt new cigarette ends,
Unhygienic, unhealthy.

Anger looks like the roaring
Fire of the poor and the homeless.

Anger feels and sounds like a funeral song,
It makes me feel sore.

Chloe Bacon (10)
Weedon Bec Primary School

FEELING SMALL

Feeling lonely,
Feeling hurt,
Feeling down
Because of one person,
She gloats in the centre of the playground,
I look away.

Sarah Hamilton (11)
St Lawrence School

FEELINGS

Today in the playground
I asked if I could play.
They said no! and called me names.
I was lonely, unwanted and angry,
All these emotions in one mind,
What should I do?
Hit them,
Tell a teacher,
Or just walk away?

Wayne Stirling (11)
St Lawrence School

IS THAT WHAT FRIENDS ARE FOR?

We used to play together everyday,
Morning 'til evening,
Spring to autumn,
But things changed.

He met a new friend,
Now he thinks I'm nothing,
Not his best friend anymore.

Summer isn't the same,
It's lonely and dull,
Not exciting and fun,
It's just not fair
I wish it was like before.

John Sharp (11)
St Lawrence School

MY FEELINGS

Shouting, screaming,
Why am I saying these things?
"I hate you!"
Stop! Stop! Stop saying these things,
"Oh just go away!"
Sad, hurt, heavy hearted,
Left out, lonely, tired even.
These are my feelings,
Angry, annoyed, wanting to hit out.

Why can't I stop this,
I want to change things.

I tried to make friends but
We just start
Shouting and screaming . . . again.

Sara Bearman (11)
St Lawrence School

JOY

To me the colour of joy is the blueness of the sky,
To me joy tastes like baked beans,
Joy looks like Centre Parcs,
Joy sounds like the stillness of the air,
It feels like the magic of Egypt
With its tall pyramids shining in the sun.

Samuel Mitchell (10)
Pitsford Primary School

FEELINGS

He picked on me
And called me names
The things he said weren't true.
Angry, sad, mad,
I felt sorry for myself,
I wanted to cry but no
I couldn't let him win.

Lee Withey (11)
St Lawrence School

HAPPINESS

Happiness is luminous yellow
And it tastes like pure lemons,
Its scent is like flowers in the garden,
Happiness looks like the sun
Going on the summer meadows,
Happiness feels like a day of fun and laughter
Condensed into a minute.

Paul Thomas (10)
Pitsford Primary School

HATE

Hate is black as night,
It tastes like black hard stale bread,
Hate smells like a bitter faded flower,
It looks like a figure in a black cloak,
Hate sounds like a lonely silence,
It feels like a strange hand on your shoulder.

Anna Rylance-Murdoch (10)
Pitsford Primary School

LONELINESS

Loneliness is a dark damp grey,
Tasting like raw fish.
It smells like cold air in a deserted street,
It sounds like a sobbing in the night,
It feels like the emptiness of a neglected house.

Lucy Eborall
Pitsford Primary School

FEAR

Fear is white,
The taste of fear is spicy,
It smells of clammy hands,
An abandoned house,
The sound of howling wolves,
Fear shocks me.

Stephane Duguet (10)
Pitsford Primary School

INVISIBLE BEAST

Lying in the bed, dark, quiet and still,
The wind makes the curtains move
And makes the ornaments wobble and tilt.
Two glaring eyes staring from the wall,
Coming from the masks hanging quite tall.
You hide under the cover, shivering, shaking through,
And you hear the wind blowing
And your heart starts to beat too,
People say it's my imagination
But I know it's really there,
People call me stupid
But I don't take any care.

Rebecca Bishop (10)
Newton Road Junior School

THE BEAST AT HOME

The beast at night,
He is following me up the stairs,
Everywhere I go in the dark
I think he's following me right there.

But when I'm tucked up in bed
Every cover over my head,
All curled,
Safe in bed.
Terrible dreams about him
thinking he's under my bed.

At last I get to sleep
dreaming about nice things,
'Til I wake up in the night.

Hovering about on the ceiling
Over my head and round my bed,
My heart is beating faster and faster
Every night he is a fight.

Amy Nickerson (9)
Newton Road Junior School

I HATE CHORES

Chores, chores, chores,
That's all I ever do.
Chores, chores, chores,
That's the very end of you!

Do the washing up for mum
Do the housework too,
Go and wipe the baby's bum
Then go and flush the loo!

Scrub the floor and clean the sink
Dust the shelves and pots,
Make the beds with clean sheets, pink,
And play with the baby lots.

Shall I water the flowers?
Shall I mow the lawn?
Shall I use my powers?
At the crack of dawn.

Claire Farmer (10)
Long Buckby Junior School

I'M MAD

I'm mad,
I'm angry,
I feel like dandy,
I feel like . . .
Squirting water
And throwing
Cream pies.
I feel like . . .
Eating lots of
Chocolate
And making
Myself feel sick,
I feel like . . .
Treading on all
The flowers!
Daffodils and snowdrops,
I'm mad.

Susan Muddiman (11)
Long Buckby Junior School

BOREDOM

Boredom is black,
My mind's up in space,
This is a very dreary place,
It smells like coal,
It feels like a hole,
And looks like an unhappy face.

Kate Harrison (10)
Long Buckby Junior School

OH NO I'M GETTING FAT!

I wish sometimes I could be so clever
About my diet, to stay thin forever,
Jogging and sweating is all I do
I'm fat and plump, it is so true.
I start to exercise, it really is good
But after that I need some pud'.
IT'S NOT FAIR I can't be thin
I can't even fit in the paper bin
I've just done some exercises and I am tired
I'm really fat, I just go tired!
Nobody likes me because I'm fat
Nobody, nobody, not even my cat.
I'm 'going' to try and exercise
I think that's really wise,
I've done it, I've done it! I really am thin
Now I don't groan
I will always GRIN!

Kiri Wilson (11)
Long Buckby Junior School

WHEN I LAY ON MY BED

When I laid on my bed
I dreamt of things I've never seen before,
Like a mouse wearing roller skates
And skating across the floor.

A tiger wearing pyjamas,
Because he had not stripes,
He got rather hot and sweaty
Especially under bright lights.

An elephant was wearing ballerina shoes
And goes with a thud, thud, thud!
She breaks the bones of lots of people
And the fragile spider leaks blood.

Frances Palmer (9)
Higham Ferrers Junior School

MY SOUL LIES STILL

My soul lies still,
Ever buried in the damp sodden earth,
My grave long forgotten yet my courage remembered.
I stay, forever's sleep with my immortal youth,
Not breathing yet living in the timeless past.
Although alone I am forgotten,
With others I am remembered.
I may have died in battle but am peaceful in death.
I lived for my country,
Fought for my country,
Died for my country,
Although surrounded by others.
I shall never see, never speak,
No noise will awake me,
No movement will stir me.
I will never awake as myself,
Though am forever being born into new life.
My heart's spirit lives in the red flower poppy,
As each seed flies my spirit goes too,
As each bud blooms
I live . . . once more.

Helen Webster (11)
Long Buckby Junior School

WHAT I LIKE BEST

What I like best
Is eating beans,
Not wearing new jeans
Or making scenes,
What I like best
Is eating beans.

Daniel Rose (8)
Denfield Park Junior School

SADNESS

Sadness is when people cut down the rainforest,
Sadness is when people die of hunger,
Sadness is when you fall out with your friend,
Sadness is when people kill elephants for ivory,
Sadness is when you watch sad programmes,
Sadness is when animals die,
Sadness is when your best friend goes to another school.
Sadness is when your brother or sister
Gets a nicer birthday present than you,
Sadness is when you don't want what you've got
For your birthday.

Rebecca Bridgens (7)
East Hunsbury Lower School

GREAT MEMORIES

My house is the granary
Where . . .

Mr Gulliver took his corn to
In 1900 . . .

In those days there were two railway lines.

In our village we had a bakery,
A butchers, a wheelwright and an undertaker.
Mr Gulliver . . .
Used the bakery a lot for the lovely hot doughnuts.

When he went to our school
His only subjects were . . .
The three Rs.

My house is the granary
Where . . .

Mr Gulliver took his corn to
In 1900

Chris Marsh (11)
Helmdon Primary School

WHEN I WAS OLD

When I was old I could not walk
I was very weak and could not talk.
When I was old I spent my life in a chair
Brushing and combing my grey white hair.
When I was old I was very slow
I wanted to watch a cricket match but could not go.

I remember my old friends how happy we were,
Now I'm stuck here in my chair,
Combing my hair.

I've now lost my eye sight,
I've got no money,
And all I can do is sit in my chair,
Combing my hair.

I wish I was young
Like I used to be,
Now I'll always be old
'Til the end of me.

Stephanie Martin (8)
East Hunsbury Lower School

I WANT TO BE . . .

I want to be a teacher
I think they're really great,
I don't want to be a doctor
That I'd really hate.
I've got to work hard
And do my very best,
I'll teach my pupils Maths and English
And won't give them many tests.
They'd better work hard
And not be naughty
Or they will be in the yard.

Sophie Clark (9)
Newton Road Junior School

WHAT I LIKE BEST

What I like best is ballet,
Yes, walking on blocks,
Not putting on socks,
But blocks,
Not locks or rocks,
But blocks.

What I like best is singing,
Yes, singing,
Not swimming or winning,
Just singing,
Not batting a ball,
Just singing.

Francesca Wales (9)
Denfield Park Junior School

CAN WE CHANGE?

Do you think we can change the world?
Some say yes
Some say no,
I think we can
If we try hard enough,
If we are kind,
If we are thoughtful to others
And share our world,
I'm going to try,
I think you should too,
Do you think life is good?
Some say yes,
Some say no,
I think it is
If we love enough,
If we try hard enough,
If we have a go at it all
And share our joy,
I'm going to try
I think you should too.

Lizzie Hill (11)
Culworth CE Primary School

I LIKE

I like my house because it's in the countryside,
How about you?
I like my pets because I can cuddle them inside and outside,
How about you?
I like my friends because they are always on my mind and always kind,
How about you?
I like my family because they look after me and let me be,
How about you?
I like my school because it teaches me things that I don't know,
How about you?

Tom Gray (11)
Culworth CE Primary School

WHEN

When I'm happy I whistle a tune,
When I'm excited I like to dance,
When I go for a jog I feel fresh,
When I'm puffed out I want to sit down,
When the winter is here I want to go outside,
The rainbow colours are beautiful.

Natalie Hale (7)
Camp Hill Lower School

DARK

It's too light
And sleep won't come,
There is a full moon
Your face goes glum,
The wind is howling
And I feel scared.
The shadows are playing,
The owls are hooting,
The cats are meowing,
The dustbins rattling.
Why won't sleep come?

Hallam Walker (6)
Cedar Road Lower School

I LOVE THE WORLD

I love this world,
I love people,
I love animals,
I love me.
I love food,
I love Tom,
I love my mum,
And she loves me.
I love singing,
In the bath,
In the car,
In assembly,
On a mountain
In York.
I love my CD Rom,
I love my friends,
Well nearly all,
I even love my sister.
I love where I live,
I love East 17,
I love this world.

Jenny Tcherniak (11)
Culworth CE Primary School

WHY BOTHER?

Why bother to be nice,
What's in it for me?

Why bother to bin litter,
What's in it for me?

Why bother to recycle things,
What's in it for me?

Why bother to follow the commandments,
What's in it for me?

Why bother to forgive,
What's in it for me?

Why bother to consider others,
What's in it for me?

Bothering to do all these things combined will make
a better life for everyone and a better world to live in.

John Henson (11)
Culworth CE Primary School

A POEM PRAYER TO MY GOD

Help me,
Help us,
Help one another
Get through the times
Of upset,
Of growing up,
Of getting old,
Of sadness,
Of death.
We need to know you are there
To help us,
Help me,
Help one another.

Gemma Trower (11)
Culworth CE Primary School

TRYING NOT TO CRY

I was wondering where he was,
Trying not to cry.
He would miss his dinner,
Cold outside,
Trying not to cry.
I was waiting,
No one to cuddle,
Trying not to cry.
Lying in bed,
Worried,
No one to keep my feet warm,
Trying not to cry.
We put an advert in the Post Office,
Tabby cat lost,
Trying not to cry.
We waited for the knock on the door,
The ring of the telephone,
We tried not to cry when no one came.

Anna Saunders (8)
Byfield Primary School

GETTING UP AND GOING TO SCHOOL

Brrrmmm! Wake up! Ohhh!
Wake up child you'll be late for school.
Don't kick the covers off your bed,
Open your curtains.
Go and wake Josh up and open his curtains.
Clomp, clomp, clomp!
Creak . . . wahhhhh!
Oh no!
Pitter patter . . .
I THOUGHT I told you to wake your brother up.
I'm going to have a fag.
Don't fiddle with your porridge!
Get ready!
Go to school!
SCHOOL.
Reading books out.
What's the matter with you Jessica?
Sit up straight, stop yawning
I hate mornings!
COMING HOME FROM SCHOOL AND TEATIMES.
Hi mum!
Have you eaten all your lunch?
Yes mum.
Ohh go and watch TV and get out of my way!
Mums! I hate 'em . . .
Teatime, eat your tea,
Mum can I have a lolly?
Not 'till after tea.
Bed time!
No! I like this programme!
I blooming well said bed, did I not?
Go to bed now!
No! I LIKE THIS PROGRAMME
No! You are at school tomorrow,
You make such a hassle when you come home!
And by the way it's got swearing in it.
Oh yes.
Now bed!
Ohhhhh!
You don't want to get up in the morning
And you don't want to go to bed!
Oh I HATE MUMS!
Don't be rude.
Yes mum heeeeeeelp!

Jessica Prestidge (7)
Byfield Primary School

TRYING NOT TO CRY

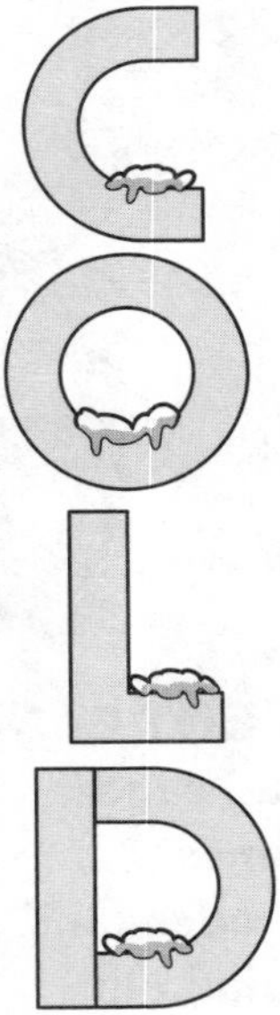

We were doing work at school
"Becky, time to go to the dentist"
That's Mrs Cross shouting,
"Come on Becky, in the car"
"Mum why do I always have to
Go to the dentist on Wednesday?"
"Here we are"
Open the door.
"Rebecca Goswell please"
That was Mrs Bell's helper,
Down the corridor into the room,
"Sit down on the chair please Becky",
I was looking at the dentist's tools,
Mrs Bell got a big needle,
Squirted it to check it.
I tried not to cry.
"Just a few little pricks"
I tried not to cry.
Mrs Bell pulled out my tooth.
I came out of the dentist
Looking happy and gappy,
I tried not to cry and I didn't.

Becky Goswell (9)
Byfield Primary School

IN THE WINTER

Freezing cold outside, winds whirling,
My whiskers twitch waiting to be let in.
Mistress and master and two children warm inside,
Let me in, someone let me in.

At last someone's let me in,
I sit down by the fire nice and warm,
I feel as if I'm having a big hug,
I watch flames jump up and down,
I'm given the leftovers of turkey from the feast,
I like being inside rather than outside.

Jessica Prestidge (7)
Byfield Primary School

TRYING NOT TO LASH OUT AT A FRIEND

Sometime last week
We were playing football
In the playground,
When I took a shot
Kyle shouted "Goal, goal".
But then he stopped the ball
And put it in the goal himself.

I was so angry
I went to the school wall
And I hit it.
He did it two more times
And I felt that he had betrayed me.
I was angry all day,
Trying not to lash out at a friend.

Nathan Grocott (9)
Byfield Primary School

GRANDAD'S GOT CANCER

My grandad had cancer
My mum was upset,
I didn't really understand
But mum and dad did.
He was sent to hospital
I was only three.
I came in shouting
"Where is he then?"
I feel guilty about that now,
But mum understood.
She left it at that.

Chloe Matic (9)
Broughton Primary School

FRIGHTENED

I'm frightened of
The dark house,
Dark nights,
Dark cupboards,
Dark stormy nights,
Dark ants,
Dark hair,
Dark eye,
Dark glasses,
Dark shed,
Dark things.

Mia Challoner (6)
Paul Munday (7)
Brixworth Primary SchooL

FEELINGS

When I'm happy I whistle a tune,
When I'm excited I like to dance,
When I go for a jog I feel fresh,
When I'm puffed out I want to sit down,
When I'm angry I make my face go red
And make fists,
When I am sad I cry,
When I am tired I lay down,
When I am lonely I feel scared.

Rachel Bunyard (7)
Camp Hill Lower School

I'M FRIGHTENED OF . . .

I'm frightened of
Fire dragons,
Red ants,
Snappy crocodiles,
Wild cats,
Poisonous snakes,
Greedy alligators,
They all bite me.

Alex Tomlins (7)
Edward Vann (7)
Brixworth Primary School

I'M FRIGHTENED OF

I'm frightened of
Being locked in the garage,
Being locked in the house with a witch,
Being lost in a street,
Being lost in the forest,
Being alone,
It's really scary.

Charlotte Walker (7)
Ben Baker (7)
Brixworth Primary School

LIFE

In all the world,
In all the streets,
I choose yours in which to sleep.
At night I sleep upon the floor
The weather, cold, I am sore.
But still I live this lonely life,
Fear of the gun, fear of the knife.
So if you find it in your soul,
A better world would make me whole.

William Farquarson (11)
Braunston CE Primary School

WHY SHOULD I?

If I get asked to wash up
Why should I?
If mum says shut up and sit
Why should I?
Dad says eat up love
Why should I?
If mum and dad say go to bed
Why should I?
But when mum and dad say go to sleep
I will
GOOD NIGHT.

Emma Halliday (9)
Barry Lower School

DON'T

Don't put your finger in the hamster's cage,
Don't go near the glasses,
Don't go on the bed,
Don't swing on the chair,
Don't be cheeky,
Don't shout at me.
So many things I mustn't,
Whatever can I do?

Thomas Causebrook (7)
Bliss Charity Aided School

IF I COULD BUY WHATEVER I WANTED . . .

If I could buy whatever I wanted
I would choose...
A rabbit that cleans itself out every day
And buys it's own food and gets its own water,
A button that would make everybody go up in the sky,
A bed that would put the quilt cover on itself,
A house that would do the housework and do the gardening,
A coat that would put itself on and do the buttons up,
A room that would clean on its own and do the windows every week.

Gemma Camp (9)
Bliss Charity Aided School

IF I COULD BUY

If I could buy whatever I wanted I would choose . .
A football that kicks itself,
A pen that does my work,
Clothes that jump on me when I wake up,
A sweet that will make me dance brilliantly,
A tree with money on it,
A swimming costume that makes me swim very fast,
A gerbil that lets me pick it up.

Amanda Boyson (8)
Bliss Charity Aided School

THE TWO SIDES OF ME

"The teacher's crying, let's make her bad,"
"No, no I said, she's really sad."

"There's a pencil, let's break the lead,"
"No, or you'll get sent to bed."

"There's a balloon, let's go and burst it,"
"No, you don't want to be a great big twit."

"Let's help mum with the dishes,"
"No, let's go and kill the fishes."

Michael Perry (8)
Barry Lower School

IF I COULD BUY WHATEVER I WANTED . . .

If I could buy whatever I wanted
I would choose . . .
A brother that takes turns
In cleaning out the rabbits,
A pencil that writes by itself,
A robot that cleans up clouds at night
For my telescope,
A plane that folds up into a suitcase,
A ghost that gets the maths answers
From the answer book,
A car that takes off
And flies to the end of traffic jams.

Lee Wilson (10)
Bliss Charity Aided School

THE TWO SIDES OF ME

"It's ten p.m., let's watch TV,"
"No, it's much too late for me."

"Let's sneak outside and go to the park,"
"No, it's getting very dark."

"Let's sneak into the kitchen and have a munch,"
"No, let's get out mum and dad's lunch."

"Let's push mum into the swimming pool,"
"No, let's go to Sunday school."

"Let's go on holiday to the Highlands,"
"No, let's buy my mum some diamonds."

"Now let's wreck dad's tapes,"
"No, let's go and do some gardening with the rakes."

"I'll pinch dad on the thumb,"
"No, you might get told off by mum."

Freddy Gilder (7)
Barry Lower School

IF I COULD BUY WHATEVER I WANTED . . .

If I could buy whatever I wanted
I would choose. . . .
A pen that writes by itself,
A dog that walks itself,
An electric teacher,
A spelling book that tells you the answers,
A clock in the classroom which always says
quarter past three,
A bike that flies wherever you want it to go,
A button which will turn people off for two hours,
A fishing rod which will always catch something big.

Dominic Stirling (9)
Bliss Charity Aided School

MY WORLD

The gentle sway of the trees,
Sun beaming down on me,
My rabbit pokes his soft nose
Out of the cage bars,
Silence.
Rustling of the leaves,
The bench is warm,
Then my brain clicks off.

I start to daydream,
I hear a faraway splashing of a stream.
Suddenly a little man appears,
"Hello" he calls,
"Here is your house sir",
The little man says in a Scottish voice.
The shimmering swimming pool flashes in the sun,
Click!

My world, my lovely world is fading away,
I start to stroke my rabbit,
And I start to daydream again.

Matthew Cartwright (9)
Barby CE Primary School

DON'T

Don't climb trees because you might fall out,
Don't forget to change,
Don't jump on the bed,
Don't tease the dogs,
Don't play football in the house,
Don't fight,
Don't eat with your mouth full,
Don't argue.
So many things I mustn't,
Whatever can I do?

Shane Hill (7)
Bliss Charity Aided School

THE TWO SIDES OF ME

"Miss isn't looking, I'll whisper to Jane,"
"No, don't you dare, it might lead to pain."

"Come on let's go and jump on the bed,"
"No, you might fall and bump your head."

"Let's go to the park,"
"No, stay inside it's too dark."

"Let's go and drive mum up the wall,"
"No, that wouldn't be nice at all."

Sarah Oakman (9)
Barry Lower School

DON'T

Don't sit on the car,
Don't jump on the bed,
Don't wear your shoes indoors,
Don't forget to change,
Don't have a midnight feast,
Don't fight with your brother,
Don't go out without your coat,
Don't snore at night.
So many things I mustn't,
Whatever can I do?

Josie Waller (8)
Bliss Charity Aided School

DON'T

Don't forget to change,
Don't slam the doors,
Don't move the table,
Don't jump on the bed,
Don't swing on your chairs,
Don't throw your clothes about,
Don't bit your nails,
Don't fight with your brother.
So many things I mustn't,
Whatever can I do?

Danielle Moore (7)
Bliss Charity Aided School

DON'T

Don't forget to change,
Don't argue,
Don't fight,
Don't sit on the TV controls,
Don't climb on the apple tree,
Don't talk with your mouth full,
Don't sit on the arms of the chairs.
So many things I mustn't,
Whatever can I do?

Alistair Hanson (8)
Bliss Charity Aided School

DON'T

Don't jump on the washing,
Don't wear shoes in the house,
Don't bounce on the bed,
Don't bounce on the settee,
Don't do cartwheels in the house,
Don't go to the woods with your shoes on,
Don't forget your lunch,
Don't forget your manners.
So many things I mustn't,
Whatever can I do?

Alexandra Needham (7)
Bliss Charity Aided School

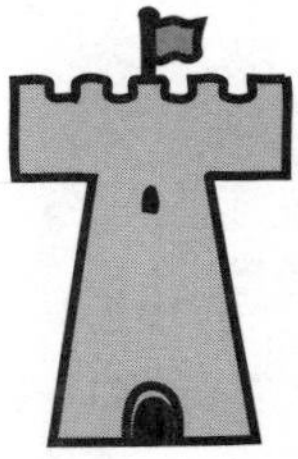

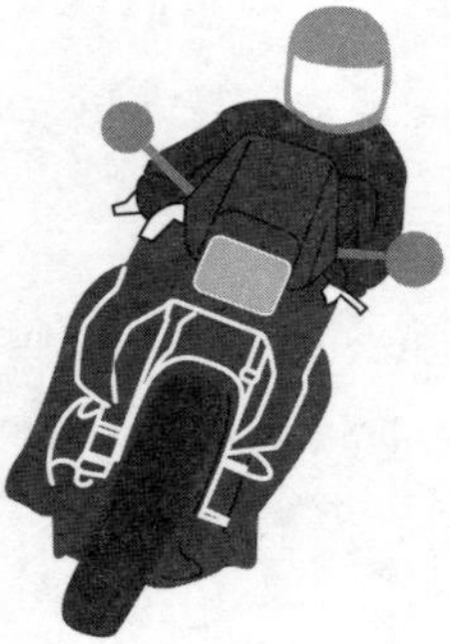

MY MOTORBIKE

When I came home one day,
I found the thing on which to play,
Standing in my garage.
This was soon to be
My new horse and carriage.
It takes to hills
Like sails to mills,
Now that's my motorbike!

This machine is orange and black,
When she starts she'll make it back.
Even in Yorkshire she will go,
Never mind the drifting snow.
But I can bet a chance in a million,
That my dear mum won't be my pillion.
'Cause she likes her feet upon the ground,
And can't abide that snarling sound!

Rachel Sawyer (11)
Weedon Bec Primary School

TRAINS

Trains go on tracks,
Rolling fast,
All the time,
I've been in a train to
Northampton.

Abbey Wiggett (5)
Redwell Infant School

TRANSPORT

Transport is fast cars,
Transport is a racing car,
Transport is a plane,
Transport is trains,
Transport is a bus,
Transport is an ice cream van,
Transport is a motorbike,
Transport is a helicopter,
Transport is a lorry.

Cheryl French (6)
Pitsford Primary School

CANALS

Come and see the boats.
At Stoke Bruerne there are lots of boats.
Never jump in.
Artists paint the boats.
Loads of lovely boats.

Big barges sail.
About 234 years ago the first canal was made.
Red boats.
Green boats.
Ever been on a boat?
Slowly the boats sail.

Vicki Wilson (7)
Higham Ferrers Junior School

TRAINS

Trains are slow,
Trains are fast,
Mallard is fast,
Diesels are slow,
Over points,
Over crossings,
Over bridges,
Through stations.

Brett Dundas (9)
Camp Hill Lower School

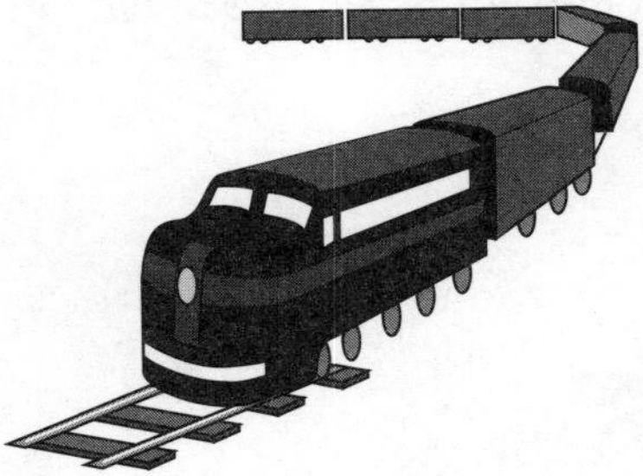

TRACTORS

Tractors are choppy
And they are smelly,
With their big chunky wheels
They wobble like jelly,
Blimey,
Grimy,
What a dirty windscreen.

Luke Johnson (9)
Camp Hill Lower School

BICYCLES

Bicycles can be big or small,
  it doesn't matter as long as it goes.

I have a bicycle with eighteen gears
  and it is big.

Cycle I can cycle very fast, I have
  a very fast bike.

You have to wear a helmet,
  unless you want to hurt yourself.

Can I fix my bike if something goes wrong?

Long journey from the park to down town.

Everyone after school, we meet
  at Spar at 4.30 p.m.

Sometimes I have a race with most of my mates,
  we start from the park and end up down the town.

Jamie Marks (10)
Newton Road Junior School

THE INVISIBLE FORCE

An invisible force,
Sparks you can't hold,
Demolishing,
Racing,
Dashing along the wire.
Thunder crashing,
Lightning crackling,
My mother's dashing home
While the lightning's flashing.
Then at that moment,
A power cut,
Everywhere is dark,
I'm terrified and frightened.
Shadows leap out from every corner of the room.
Next day it's colourful and bright,
The storm has gone.
The best thing is,
Our house hasn't been touched at all.

Luke Graham (8)
Whitefriars Junior School

RAIN

Splash
Splash
Splashing,
I like jumping in
Puddles.

Kerry White (6)
Bliss Charity Aided School

THE RAIN

Splashing, splashing,
In the puddles,
Mum I'm soaking wet!

Thomas Brewster (6)
Bliss Charity Aided School

SNOWY MORNING

A slippery, cold morning,
The snow swirling as it falls.
Soft powdered plants weaken.
The wind whirling past you,
Cold fingers tingling.
Snowball fights wherever you go,
People getting covered in snow.
Morning crisp air is all quiet.

Kimberly Scarrott (10)
Bliss Charity Aided School

RAIN

Rain dripping
From the sky,
We all get wet.

Rory Smallbone (6)
Bliss Charity Aided School

SNOWY MORNING

A hazy morning, the world is quiet,
The curtains out of focus.
On the pane is the dazzling world of white,
Shining in your face, your sleepiness is gone.
You rush downstairs, a hurried breakfast,
Orange juice all over the floor.
You jump into your boots, rush outside,
A waving scarf, a half put on coat,
A pair of boots.
All sprinting along in the crisp morning,
The scrunching and crackling snow
Beneath your feet.
A snowball fight, freezing missiles
Shoot through the air,

Cold and dishevelled you build a snowman.
Your sledge is worn out too,
Then the morning has passed.

Robin Newstead (9)
Bliss Charity Aided School

SNOWY MORNING

I look outside, it's all plain white,
I dress up warm and go outside.
There's millions of footprints
In the crisp snow,
There's snowball fights
Wherever you go.
Building snowmen, having fun,
Sledging down slidy drives.
Children skidding, falling over,
Getting covered in snow like a snowman.
It's time to go in,
Your fingers sting,
What a day!

Laura Wise (10)
Bliss Charity Aided School

WATER

Splish,
Splosh,
Splash,
The rain is coming down
From the sky.

Jamie Devlin (6)
Bliss Charity Aided School

SNOW IN BRIXWORTH

Cold, wet and white,
They are the words that go
Through my mind when I pull
Back the curtain to see snow,
Beautiful snow falling muffled
To the ground slowly but surely
Melting,
Quietly
Melting.

Christopher Wright (10)
Brixworth Primary School

RAIN

Rain splashes,
Rain falls on the ground,
I like jumping in the puddles.

Anthony Garrett (6)
Bliss Charity Aided School

LIGHTNING

First comes the darkness,
Then the sky is lit
By the shock of lightning.
Silence,
Then boom, bang!
Trees catching fire.
The rain belting on our windows,
Shock when all the lights go off,
Running around finding candles
And searching for matches.
The wind
Whistles through cracks in the windows.
Then the lightning stops,
Out comes the sun
As the storm moves on.

Adam Carr (8)
Whitefriars Junior School

THE RAIN

Drip,
Drop,
Drip,
Drop,
The rain falls down on the cars.

Jonathan Haynes (6)
Bliss Charity Aided School

DRIZZLY

Drizzly, it is raining,
Drizzly, it is raining,
Drizzly, it is raining,
I am in my den.

Nicola Stevenson (7)
Bliss Charity Aided School

THE RAIN

Splish,
Splash,
Splish,
Splash,
The rain is coming
From the cloud.

James Garlick (6)
Bliss Charity Aided School

SUGAR SNOW

Untouched white, sugar snow,
Clear cut, silent and immaculate.
Prints in the opaque blanket of white,
Wonder at what stories they tell.
A beautiful vision in silver,
Specks of sparkling glitter.
On the trees, lacy ice,
Translucent drops of frozen water.
Snow for infinity,
An endless sheet of icing.
Blue shadows of images,
Some motionless or dead.
A foggy mist of breath,
Brings out the crispness in the air.

Sun rising on the horizon,
Touches shadowy places.
Withdrawn hard ice,
Is softened in the glow.
Trees carrying majestic glaring snow,
Natural green servants.
Glassy ponds,
Of frozen waters.
Blue sky is shining,
So clean and so blue.
New impressions are starting to form,
In the soft glistening snow.

Rebecca Hammond (11)
Weedon Bec Primary School

SNOWSTORM

I like snow so white and bold,
It covers the ground all crisp and cold.

I like a storm of heavy snow,
We all get stuck – nowhere to go.

Look out of the window and see it fall,
Build a snowman soon; big, fat and tall.

Tyrone Doyle (8)
Weedon Bec Primary School

CLOUDS

I see the clouds
Rushing by
Like cotton wool,
White and fluffy,
Making me dizzy
As they pass by.
Grey and stormy now,
Dragon shapes are now swaying trees,
Horses changing into angry faces.
I see the clouds
Rushing by.

Eamonn Morrison (7)
St Brendan's Infant School

WHITE DUST

White dust is falling slowly.
It reminds me of a flying albino squirrel.
When it's fresh and I step in it,
It feels like a deep trap.

Luke Slack (8)
St Lawrence School

SNOW

The glare of the sun on the snow
brightens the day,
Your feet crunch in the opaque ice
and make big marks.
You see your shadow long and thin,
blue and still,
The pond is still and covered with fine ice,
Throw some snow, it will crack
into little crystals of ice.
Snow is like a blanket of sugar,
It breaks in your hands
and makes them cold.
Icicles hang from small delicate trees
on the side of a country lane.

Laura Oakey (11)
Weedon Bec Primary School

SNOW
Snow is freezing.
Lovely and fresh.
Snow is like a rabbit
And my soft bed.
Snow glides down in waves.
It is crispy and agile.
Snow is like bags of white flour
Falling from the sky.
Sarah Bolton (8)
St Lawrence School

WEATHER CHANGES
The weather changes,
Night changes to day,
Rain changes to snow,
Snow changes to water again,
Wind changes your hair,
The grass changes with it.
Karen Maley (7)
Redwell Infant School

RAIN
Raindrops making puddles,
And I am under my umbrella.
Inside getting dry near the fire,
Now it's going to rain again,
drip, drip, drip.
Roxanne Brenkley (7)
St Brendan's Infant School

CHANGING WEATHER
The sky changes,
Blue and grey,
Sometimes it snows.
The wind rushes round you.
Sometimes it rains,
You get wet
And you go home.
Andrew Ward (7)
Redwell Infant School

A WONDERLAND OF SNOW

A woven white roof thatched with snow.
A mountain peak, sparkling like sugar.
It's a wonderland.

A big hill, almost above the sky.
A white duvet in the blinding sun.
An amazing wonderland of snow

Yesterday all those things were there.
But the sun came out and it's gone.
The snow has gone.

Rory Aitkenhead (9)
Newnham Primary School

SNOW

It snowed on Friday.
I made a snowman.
I threw snowballs at my daddy.
I fell over.
Snow is very soft.
Snow is very beautiful.
Snow drips and it makes water.

Sarah Hadley (5)
Pitsford Primary School

SNOW

The fields look like a glittering white duvet,
A snow queen's cloak.
Trees stand out like spiky ice monsters,
One like the Ice King with its flower babies
Bowing their golden heads.
The roofs are thatched
With a glistening blanket of snow.
Icicles hang like the fangs of an ice beast,
With its saliva dripping off them
As tinkling clear water.

Cian Motley (11)
Newnham Primary School

SNOW DAY IN NEWNHAM

The roofs are covered
With a white glistening carpet.
The icicles hang from the houses
Like silver daggers waiting to drop.

The trees wave their white, silk covered
Arms to the sky.
The fields are like a diamond quilt.
The sheep stand as if frozen.
If you moved one it would crack.

The road is like a wide, glittery river,
Which the cars have torn asunder.

The snow does not stay forever.
It will all soon be gone.
It will run down the road as a rapid,
Like something that has never existed.

Kate Dugan (11)
Newnham Primary School

LET'S BE TINY SNOWFLAKES

Let's be tiny snowflakes
And fall gently from the sky,
Make a snow white carpet
Without making any sound.

Let's be Jack Frost
With his sweeping broom,
And make tiny patterns
On every windowsill.

Let's be a snowman
With a pipe, gloves and scarf,
So white and so cold,
And when the sun comes out to play
We quickly run away.

Stevie Kramer (9)
Lumbertubs Lower School

RAIN

Rain is splashing in puddles,
Wet rainy days.
Rain is going out to play,
Wet rainy days.
Rain is pitter patter on the window,
Wet rainy days.
Rain is jumping muddy water,
Wet rainy days.
Rain is wearing my mac,
Wet rainy days.

Victoria Martin (6)
East Hunsbury Lower School

A WEATHER POEM

Windy, foggy, cold
And very snowy.
Wet and damp,
Who cares if it's raining?
Cloudy, cold,
Icy dull and wet.
Sleet, lightning,
Thunder very frightening.
Frosty, gales, breezy,
Please, some summer weather.
Sun, brightness,
Warmth, thank you!

Kevin Touhey (8)
East Hunsbury Lower School

LET'S BE SNOWFLAKES

Freezing cold icicles
Hanging from the roof,
Sparkling ice.
More snow is falling down
To the ground,
All pretty and white.
It feels cold
Soft like cotton wool.
Frosty, freezing, snowy
And sometimes slushy.

Amanda Holton (8)
Lumbertubs Lower School

THE DIFFERENT WEATHER

The wind is howling outside
And my father sighed and sighed,
"Oh dear", he said,
"I am going to bed,
For I am awfully dizzy".

The rain is pattering down
And I am wearing a gown,
That is keeping me warm,
That I'll wear 'till dawn,
"Goodnight everyone here!"

The sun is outside shining
And my brother kept on lying,
He said, "It was wet",
I said "I bet!"
But he said, "I was wrong, so there!"

There's a hurricane brewing up,
I could catch it in a cup,
For it is so, so small,
That I could even crawl
Right up next to it.

There's a thunderstorm in the sky
And I am going to cry,
For I am afraid
That we will fade
Away into the storm.

Claire Farmer (10)
Long Buckby Junior School

THE SNOW

White and flaky,
The snow stands clear
For all to see.
It's so perfect,
So peaceful.

Glimmering white,
As smooth as a feather,
Dancing like a ballet,
Coming down thick and fast.

In the morning the town
Is covered in white,
As soft and slushy,
It feels like paradise.

Nicholas Larmour (9)
Havelock Junior School

RAIN

Welly boots in the puddles.
An umbrella day, pitter patter.
Drizzling on my knee.
Rainy days.

Sploshing on my window.
Splashing in the water.
Plopping on my mac.
Rainy days.

Flowers to grow.
Ducks' favourite weather.
Falling from the sky.
Rainy days.

Jenny Cooper (7)
East Hunsbury Lower School

SNOW IN BRIXWORTH

The snow covers trees
As a woman walks past with her dog.
Droplets of half frozen water
Glide down while ecstatic children
Play in the streets, like hungry mice
When they see a pile of seeds.
The snow has brought silence to the world.
However, the ice blanket can't last forever.
So when it comes enjoy it while you can.
Sarah, my elder sister, comes to see us
While the snow is on the ground.
I like to watch our dog chase snowflakes
In the garden.
Each time it snows and I go out into the
Streets of Brixworth,
Ecstasy grows inside me.
Snow has covered the ground again,
So let's enjoy it.

Rebecca Wilsdon (10)
Brixworth Primary School

SNOW IN BRIXWORTH

When I woke up,
There on the ground
Lay a blanket that covered
All around.

Cotton wool lay on the road,
Glittering flakes
Swivelled and swirled.

The world was in quietness,
Silent as can be,
All you could see
Was the white breath of me.

Gemma Claydon (10)
Brixworth Primary School

WATER

Drip, drip, dripping,
Splash, splash, splashing,
In the puddles.

Laura Poole (6)
Bliss Charity Aided School

SNOW IN BRIXWORTH

It's time to play,
The fun is just beginning.
It's like confetti hesitating as it falls.
It makes you forget wars and fights.
The snow on the trees bends its branches.
As I look out of the window I want to go and feel it.
Then the chance I've been waiting for,
I can go out.
As I run to touch and taste
All my hopes lift.

Leonie Harwood (10)
Brixworth Primary School

THE MEASLES JAB

I went to have my jab,
I went in with my chest out
And my muscles up.
I said to myself
I am not scared.
I went in,
They put the needle into me.
I said to myself that hurt!
Then I showed off.

Andrew Overton (8)
Barby CE Primary School

WOBBLY TOOTH

It's just perching there on my gum
Like a rock wobbling on a mountain,
Or a bell hanging there,
Swinging to and fro,
My friendly companion.
I've always liked it,
Probably always will,
Until it plops off
My big red rubbery gum,
Like a white raindrop falling.

Tamara Lawrence (9)
Barby CE Primary School

GOOSE BUMPS

I look at my goose bumps,
I really hate them.
They are all sticking up on my arms,
They make me think of a plucked bird.
They are always ready to come up,
Even when I think of an apple.
They jump out on me,
It makes me jump.
I wish I could chop them off.

David England (8)
Barby CE Primary School

A CANDLE BURNING

The dancing flames,
The scent of wax.
Grey smoke haunts the air,
Dripping, melted wax slides.
The wicked green of flame and fire
Wipes out the curse of burning,
Darkness fills the room.

Lance Pursey (8)
Barry Lower School

MY GANGLION

The fat squashy ganglion
Hangs on my wrist.
Everytime my hand goes back
It pops out again like a bold jack-in-the-box.
The ganglion looks like a block of snow
Falling off a cliff,

BUT IT WON'T FALL!

Louisa Walsh (9)
Barby CE Primary School

MEASLES INJECTION

My name gets called,
I walk in.
I shiver.
She tells me to look at her,
I glare and glare.
She stabs the needle in,
Then she pulls it out,
It feels slimy.
I walk out, then into the classroom,
Everyone wants to look at my arm.
I look at it, it has spots on.
I don't understand,
The sticker says no spots.

Carrie McGeoch (8)
Barby CE Primary School

GO OPEN THE DOOR

Go and open the door,
Outside there may be . . .
Potato birds riding jelly bikes
On a treacle river.

Cherry flavoured trees riding
Marshmallow elephants whilst
Singing nursery rhymes backwards.

Feet doing their homework
And eating glue bread
With soggy semolina on.

Burned sausages
Bungee jumping
Whilst making saucepan casserole.

Hamsters playing baseball
On rollerboots.
Go open the door,
At least there will be a draught.

Danielle Massingham (10)
Bliss Charity Aided School

MUSIC FREAK

I do music every day,
I do too much some people say,
I love all the instruments, I do,
To me I play lots too few,
I go to music school every week,
What can I say but I'm a music freak.

Sarah Clark (11)
Braunston CE Primary School

THE DARK CREAKS

The dark creaks,
Creak creak,
Trees breaking,
Creak, creak,
Door swings,
Creak, creak,
Dark.

Ryan Roberts (6)
Cedar Road Lower School

GO AND OPEN THE DOOR

Go and open the door,
Outside there may be . . .
A crazy yellow rubber bike
And the seat is made out of toffee,
A cardboard tree with Mars
Growing on them, drinking
Spotty milkshake,
A lamppost, dancing to 'Away In A Manger'
And eating holes in dogs,
A tin of baked beans drinking cherry soda
And dancing to 'Jingle Bells',
The snow is whipped ice cream
With spotty dots on,
Walnuts rolling down the bread spotty hill.
Go and open the door,
At least there will be a draught.

Rachel Bristow (9)
Bliss Charity Aided School

BEING TOLD OFF

I begin to shiver,
My shoulders clutch together.
Fire eyes stare at me,
Hands by her sides.
"Why are you on the grass?" she whispers.
My eyes turn to look at the ground,
I stare and stare,
Then,
"I'm sorry".
"Wait 'till last",
Mrs Davies says.

Louisa Walsh (9)
Barby CE Primary School

DOWNFALL OF A COCONUT

I hear – the owner,
I feel – the wooden ball,
I see – the coconut on it's pole,
I smell – victory,
I taste – my coconut.

David Conlin (10)
Braybrooke School

THE VIEW FROM MY WINDOW

I pull back the soft pink curtains
And look outside,
Over fields there lies a layer of snow
Under the misty air.
I tie my curtains back
And put on my dressing gown and slippers
And make my way downstairs.
I step outside, my feet crunching the snow
As I walk down the garden path.
I can feel the fresh air blowing gently in my face,
I am going to fetch the ice cold milk.
I make my way back up the path
And into the kitchen.

Alex Buckby (10)
Broughton School

GHOSTS

One night when it's dark,
Cats scream, dogs bark,
The stars shone bright,
T'was a cold, dark night.
From the house on the hill
There came a sudden shrill!
It gave me a fright,
And as I turned on the light
There was a scary ghost,
I could only scream at the most.
Shall I get up or stay in bed?
Or am I imagining it all in my head,
Shall I call mum or shall I call dad?
Or am I really going mad?
Or shall I take another peep?
On second thoughts I'll go to sleep.

Laura Britchford (9)
Denfield Park Junior School

CHRISTMAS TIME ROOM

Decorations twinkling like a candle flame
Flickering small in the light of our world,
Reflecting colours bright through our world
Tinsel reflecting the silky bed of cold white snow
Outside covering ground and trees.
A burning fire by the beautifully decorated Christmas tree,
Shining light so bright with red, yellow, blue and orange flames.
Presents lying under the tree waiting to be opened,
Wrapped in so many different colours of paper,
In all different shapes and sizes.

Hannah Galvin-Home (10)
Byfield Primary School

DON'T DO THAT!

Don't do that to next door's cat
And don't put that in aunty's hat
And don't put footprints on my mat
And don't call your little sister fat,
Don't hit your brother
With a baseball bat
And that is that!

Carly Harris (8)
Crick Primary School

RACISM

Why do people laugh and call names,
To those who are black?
What have they done?
They don't deserve to be treated badly
Just because they're black.
People shout, "Oi, YOU ,yes YOU!
The one over there,
You Paki, the one with the frizzy hair!"
Why should they suffer?
Just think before you shout.
How would you like it if it was you?

Vicky Boyle (11)
Crick Primary School

HANDS

Busy hands make a casserole,
Clever hands juggling,
Gentle hands stroking a dog,
Sad hands wiping tears away,
Happy hands playing,
Naughty hands pulling hair,
Angry hands knocking people over,
Kind hands pushing a trolley,
Helpful hands getting things from shelves,
My hands are kind and helpful.

Andrew Pepper (7)
Crick Primary School

PANDORA'S POEM

Go in the room Pandora,
Open up the box,
Go in,
Go in.

There's something for you,
Lovely jewels and smelly balls,
Go in,
Go in.

Snakes and skates,
Bats and cats,
Go in,
Go in.

Open up the box,
Ahhh!

Patricia Thompson (9)
East Hunsbury Lower School

THE CANDLE FLAME

Flickery bright,
As wicked as a finger,
As thin as a pin,
As tall as a match.
Burning the wax
Like burning wood,
As fidgety as a child,
Uncomfortable like
A man in a jail.
Changing shape
While it burns,
In a bad mood,
Melting like gooey
Chocolate.

James Kearney (9)
East Hunsbury Lower School

THE EXPLOSION

Siren sounding loud and clear,
Rumbling trembling,
"Evacuate", people shout,
Grey ash pouring down,
Covering the ground.
People scared,
Choking, coughing, crying, crowds,
Flashing, booming, thunderstorms.

A crashing boom,
Explosion!
Lava bursting out like hot raspberry sauce,
Red, bubbling, black smoke bursting out,
In a mushroom in the sky.
Pitch black day like a black cat's coat,
Everywhere black and white film,
Slippery lava stops, turns hard.

Completely changed landscape,
Mud rivers, swamp overflow,
Polluted, poisoned, petrified people,
Carrying on, everywhere destroyed.

Rachel Chapman (10)
Havelock Junior School

RUSH HOUR

Like an ants' nest,
Full of heat and power,
Noise coming from everywhere,
Stopping every now and then,
Never resting,
But by the time it's all calmed down
You can only wait 'till five!

Victoria Selby (9)
Higham Ferrers Junior School

MORTAL KOMBAT II

What moves does Kitana hide?
How does Sub-zeo do his slide?
How does Liu Kang do a bicycle kick?
Can you finish them off with just one flick?
Do Baraka and Mileena love each other?
And just what background does Johnny Cage cover?
Does Shang-Tsung obey his master?
This time is Raiden really faster?
Shao-Kahn is really cool!
Scorpion is a right old fool!
Can Kung-Lao pull rabbits from his hat?
What do people feel like when reptiles spat?
Kintaro has four arms or does he have three?
Jax uses all his strength and then does a knee!

Alistair Bloomer (10)
Long Buckby Junior School

A DROP OF POETRY

Cool and clear,
Soft and sheer,
Flowing past my skin,
Water ripples everywhere,
Cooling to my limbs,
I'm so relaxed,
I feel as if
My body is not real,
I now know what it must be like
To be a shiny seal.

Lisa Taylor (10)
Long Buckby Junior School

RINGING OUT

Ring, ring, ring goes the bell,
Screaming through the mist,
Telling the children to come,
Telling the children to listen.
Cold, grey metal shines
Inside the old tower,
Ringing for happiness,
Ringing for joy,
Watching us every hour,
Letting us know
You are there.

Emily Wood (10)
Newton Road Junior School

THE RUMOURS

I'd heard many a rumour about my new school,
Each one seeming horribly true,
Which just seemed worse than the prison-like rules,
And the thought of being new.

Last night I hadn't slept a wink,
From thinking of my new school,
About the tales warning me, I think,
To never break a rule.

They say half the teachers are mad scientists,
Using kids for experiments you see,
While the other half are wild, weird beasts,
Who eat kids just like you and me.

Though when I heard that, I just shook my head,
No one believes in that stuff,
It's like thinking a spirit will rise from the dead,
It's poppycock, dumbness and bluff.

Still though, they kept on speaking,
Though this time they moved to our head,
He bites every child 'stead 'a' beating,
For he is a vampire, they said.

And any child who enters his room,
Is never seen again,
For any child who breaks a rule,
He'll bite until they're dead!

Now I didn't really believe those things,
Though the next day I followed each rule,
And made sure I wore my garlic string,
And made sure there were lights in the school.

I don't remember anything after that,
About the vampires and beasts I'd feared,
I'd just laid my head on the table flat,
And fell asleep, it appears!

Helen Webster (11)
Long Buckby Junior School

SMELLY SOCKS!

Your socks are smelly,
Very smelly,
Your socks are smelly Nelly!

Our hamster died,
Take a guess at the cause,
Your socks are smelly Nelly!

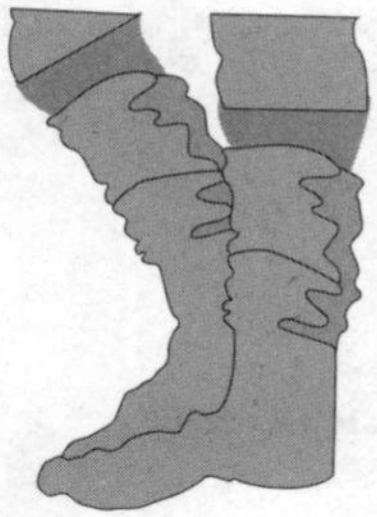

Your socks are smelly,
Very smelly,
Your socks are smelly Nelly!

Our house blew up,
Gas explosion they said,
Your socks are smelly Nelly!

Your socks are smelly,
Very smelly,
Your socks are smelly Nelly!

Nicky Brayn (9)
Long Buckby Junior School

THE WATCHFUL EYE

Snowdrops glow and grow
From sweet sugar sprinkled frost.
The mystical, magical flowers
Sit and watch for hours
The brittle ice that cracks and crunches
And rumbles in the sacred silence of the snow.
Night lingers
On and on,
Suddenly it is gone
The glinting stars,
The almighty moon,
Still the flowers
Strewn across
The now muddy ground
Watch in silence all around.

Fiona Harley (10)
Newton Road Junior School

GERMS

The germs come creeping in the night
And give you all a horrible fright,
When you wake up with lots of spots
Which turn out to be pink polka-dots!
They're big and squishy,
Small and round,
They'll invade but make no sound.
So when you wake on Christmas Day,
You will find they've come to stay,
They will get in your insides,
'Cos that is where they like to hide.
Like tapeworms they will eat your food
Because it is already chewed,
And the little entamoeba
Will give you quite a nasty fever,
And the parasitic little beasts
Eat your insides, they have a feast!
So wash your hands with every meal,
So that you will really feel
Very healthy, very fit,
You must avoid getting bit
By a creature which could carry a disease,
Such as tiny rat fleas.

Andrew Woolley (11)
Long Buckby Junior School

GOODBYE HELLO

Goodbye barbecues
Oranges
Orangeade
Drinking cold drinks
Bye summer flowers
Yellow petals
Eating cold food

Hello heating
Eating hot food
Lying in bed all cosy and warm
Lights
Olympics.

Craig Skinner (9)
Newton Road Junior School

TIMES HAVE CHANGED

Times have changed from then to now,
Boring then,
Exciting now,
Slow cars then,
Fast cars now,
Clothes have changed from then to now.

Times have changed from then to now,
Soldiers dead and us healthy specimens alive,
Vera Lynn then, Oasis now,
But I'm glad that I'm alive now
And not then.

Emily Brunton (10)
Long Buckby Junior School

GROWING UP

First we are babies,
We grow into toddlers,
And then into schoolgirls and boys,
Then into adults,
Doing their work.

Laura Smith (7)
Redwell Infant School

MONSTERS

Monsters
Slimy, scary
It eats you
It scares me
Beast.

Daniel Scott (8)
Newton Road Junior School

A LONG TIME AGO

A long time ago,
Not a lot of people had cars,
Only rich people had cars,
They had to wind up the car
To start it,
They had to put up the roof
To keep the rain off,
We don't do any of those now

Robyn Allen (7)
Redwell Infant School

THE WINDOW

Through the window there is a playground
Next to the playground there is the Infant School,
Below the window is a wall,
Outside the window is a garden,
Beside the window is a calendar,
Underneath the calendar is a computer,
Near the computer is another computer,
Next to the computer is a cupboard,
In front of the computer is a table,
Under the table is a chair,
On each side of the window there are
Two grey curtains.

Kirsti Jones (8)
Newton Road Junior School

NEW YEAR'S RESOLUTION

I will get better at comedy
Ha
Ha
Ha,
He
He
He,
Ho
Ho
Ho.

Mark Smith (8)
Rectory Farm Lower School

TEDDY BEARS

Teddy bears have changed,
They used to have straw,
They had long arms
And pointed noses,
They also had metal inside,
They had different paws,
I've got lots of new bears.

Natalie Learmouth (7)
Redwell Infant School

VIKING RAIDS
Longships on the shore
Men climb out onto the beach
Soon to raid and rob.

VIKING LANDS
Cold and miserable
Snow and rain on the mountains
Little farmland there.
James Reynolds (8)
St Andrew's CE Primary School

MORNING SOUNDS
Curtains pulled back scruffily,
Cereal packet crunching,
Water splashing as I brush my teeth,
Stairs creaking as we go up and down,
Door creaking as we go in and out,
Toilets flushing,
Letters coming through the door,
Bags and coats being zipped up,
Cars going along the road,
People chattering in the street,
Children shouting as they play football.
Claire Meadows (9)
St Andrew's CE Primary School

SHOUTING
I sat on the bench,
Sad and unwanted.
People walked by and looked at me.
I felt the lump in my throat,
I held back the tears.
I wished I could change
The things I had said.
I know that was unkind,
I hurt her feelings.
Carla Ward (11)
St Lawrence School

WHAT IS?

What is the moon?
A dusty angel glowing over me.
A crystal ball.
A giant football.
What is a book?
A tree.
A lump of wood.
A piece of wood writing.

Megan Littlechild (8)
South End Junior School

THE VAMPIRE

The vampire
Frightening
Scary
Looking for blood
The awful vampire.

Sarah Lord (8)
Newton Road Junior School

MORNING SOUNDS

Curtains swishing back,
Water splashing while brushing my teeth,
Doors creaking slowly,
Lunchboxes banging hard,
Bags zipping up quickly,
Perfume spraying,
Hair brushing,
My sister shouting,
Toilets flushing,
Coats crunching,
Cars driving along the road,
Coffee pouring,
Friends knocking,
Shoes tightening,
Laces pulling,
Everybody talking,
Lights switching off,
Mum kissing me goodbye.

Nicky Barber (9)
St Andrew's CE Primary School

VIKING LONGSHIP

Ships rowed by Vikings
Winds blew and the waves spluttered
And the longship swayed.

VIKING BATTLE

Ships are on the shore
Foes climb out in their armour
Vikings are ready.

William Chan (8)
St Andrew's CE Primary School

MORNING SOUNDS

Dad getting up at 7 o'clock,
Dad putting on the TV,
My hamster on its wheel,
My dog barking,
My brother shouting,
The bath running,
Curtains being tugged back,
Cereal packets rattling,
Crunching of cornflakes,
Eating crunchy toast.

Ruth Acaster (8)
St Andrew's CE Primary School

MORNING SOUNDS

Mum is shouting,
The toast is rattling,
The cereal box scrunching,
Crisps rattling,
The milkman tapping his feet,
The shower is pouring,
The doors slamming,
The television up full blast,
The cars going past,
The cupboards banging,
Dad snoring,
The cat meowing.

Ryan Wilson (8)
St Andrew's CE Primary School

MORNING SOUNDS

Yawning sleepily, getting out of bed,
Curtains drawn back carefully,
Splashing water while having a wash,
Cereal packets torn open,
Crunchy buttered toast eaten,
Kettle water boiled hot ready to drink,
Zipping up bags ready to take to school,
Buckled up shoes, moaning they're too tight,
Flushing loos after you've gone,
Slamming doors,
Rushing to school,
Children running with banging shoes,
Unzipping coats, chucked on the floor,
Ringing bells,
Shouting children rushing to their class.

Lisa Barber (9)
St Andrew's CE Primary School

WHAT IS?

A rabbit is a running fur ball.
The sun is a splodge of yellow paint.
The moon is a flying saucer.
A nose is a fly's ski slope.

Katie Loake (7)
South End Junior School

FIRE

A cigarette left alight,
It burst into flames in the night.
Mother calling childrens names,
Before the bedrooms go in flames.
999,
We hope the firemen get here in time.
Mother still calling children's names.
When the fire is out,
Mummy said she will shout,
"I will not smoke again!"

Eamonn Morrison (7)
St Brendan's Infant School

BUBBLES

B is for bubbles floating in the air,
U is for under, the bubble is there,
B is for bus bubbles floating down the bubble roads,
B is for bubbles hitting the floor, POP!
L is for large bubbles crushing the little ones,
E is for eager bubbles keen to get down,
S is for small bubbles spinning around.

Richard Kerr (8)
South End Junior School

VICTORY

Wind blows through the trees
Like a hot knife through butter,
The war had started.

Bombing all night long,
Will it ever stop?
Cities being destroyed.

Our dad comes home
With a laugh and a smile,
We've won the war for Europe.

Peter Swinhoe (11)
Whitefriars Junior School

MY TEETH

My teeth are white
And very bright.

I brush them twice a day
So the decay would go away,
I look after my teeth.

I've got a perfect smile
And don't have to buy
False teeth in a pile,
I look after my teeth.

I don't eat a lot of sugary stuff,
So my teeth are hard and tough,
I look after my teeth.

DO YOU?

Amy Edwards (9)
St Lawrence School

BONFIRE NIGHT

Bonfire night when the fireworks are alight,
CRASH BANG! Gold and purple sparkles.
On bonfire night there's lots of excitement,
The catherine wheel, a whizz of fire rockets zooming.
Hotdogs and poor old burning Guy and lots to do
and sparklers and stars,
Fountains of loads of colours, purple, green, red and gold,
Lots of sparklers are sold!
I love bonfire night, the roaring fire
with black smoky breath, it could put some people to death,
Raining colours so bright and fiery.
Eating is lovely because of all the smells and tastes,
Nuggets and chips, sausages and beans
and lots of beautiful scenes.
Icy fireworks with silver rays and beams,
Gold, purple, green, silver, blue, turquoise, violet and indigo.
Hills all around and on one is the fire,
Watch as the rockets go higher and higher.
Now the fireworks are over and it's time to go home.

Jack Hartwell (8)
South End Junior School

BATTLESHIP

Like a huge iron pencil case
Floating on the sea,
The huge battleship is waiting to fire.
Huge guns shooting at the enemy,
The captain giving orders,
Sailors ready to aim.
Engines are jogging about
And pumping out smoke.
Tomorrow we might be drowning
Or we could be cheering.

Michael Beckett (10)
South End Junior School

PARCEL

There's a parcel,
There's a parcel,
Outside the front door,
Could it be what
I've been waiting for?
Is it from Santa Claus?

William Teuton (8)
Southfield Primary School

MY SHADOW

My shadow follows me everywhere I go,
Over a bridge,
Across a grassy meadow.

I can jump over puddles,
My shadow can too.
Even though he lands in them,
He's never wet through.
When the sun goes in,
My shadow goes away.
But I know he'll visit me,
Another sunny day.

Alexandra Scott (7)
Weedon Bec Primary School

THE VICTORIAN WAY

Weary workers wander through
The unhealthy industrial air,
The gloomy atmosphere
Fills people with depression,
Small, unnoticed children die of diseases,
Others just don't care.
Steamy, smoggy trains
Pass through the dense atmosphere,
The ground is wet and the air is damp,
Factories barely seen
Through their own polluted smoke.

Kathryn Hudswell (11)
Southfield Primary School

PUPPETS

Puppets like to play in puppet shows,
Clowns wearing big red bows,
Stick or string, the fun never ends,
Watch them dance, sit and bend.

Gary Hopkins (6)
Ross Dove (6)
Waynflete Infant School

CRACKERS

When I open a Christmas cracker
I can't wait for the surprise,
I can hear a bang and a squeal,
I read the joke,
Put on my hat,
And look at my surprise.

Tara Dancer (9)
Southfield Primary School

MY WINDOW

When I look out of my window
This is what I see,
All the little daffodils
Bowing their heads at me.

When I look out of my window
This is what I see,
All the little birds
Sitting in our tree.

When I listen at my window
This is what I hear,
The trains are getting closer
So very very near.

When I listen at my window
This is what I hear,
I hear the church bells ringing
Very loud and very clear.

Rebecca Hawkey (7)
Weedon Bec Primary School

MY BEAR

My teddy bear is soft and brown,
His heart is warm and good,
No matter how I've hurt him,
He's always understood.

He sits upon my bed all day,
As happy as can be,
He won't get into mischief,
As he'll soon be seeing me.

When I come home from school each day,
It's a cuddle that I'm after,
There he sits, waiting for me,
So full of love and laughter.

My teddy bear is soft and brown,
His fur is wearing thin,
Each night when bedtime comes around,
There's always room for him.

Laura Hawkey (9)
Weedon Bec Primary School

WATER

Water is wet,
Sometimes hot.
Fishes like to live in it,
So do dolphins too.

Becky Bedding (5)
Weedon Bec Primary School

VICTORY FOR BRITAIN

Death and destruction,
And then a win for Britain,
Victory at last.

Soldiers return home,
Dancing and celebrations,
The war is over.

Father home at last,
Tears of joy and happiness,
Love and emotion.

Paul Munro (11)
Whitefriars Junior School

BALLOON FESTIVALS

Mum said in the morning
That it's early bed,
But we went to the
Balloon festival instead!

Shows, sweets and teddies
Were not near free,
But they said I was special
So they gave them to me!

Glowing coloured fireworks
Sparkling here and there,
We bought lots of choc'
Without a care!

So on a boring day
Why not ask your mum
To go to the balloon festival
I assure you it's fun!

Emma Bullock (8)
Cedar Road Lower School

BALLOON FESTIVALS

In the night the balloons take flight
In lots of different shapes and sizes.
There's Sonic, Mr Men, Mr Blobby
And lots and lots of others.
They fly higher and higher.

Mitchell Pink (8)
Cedar Road Lower School

MANCHESTER UNITED

Manchester United
Excellent
Great
They score goals
The winning team.

Rebecca Pinnock (8)
Newton Road Junior School

INDEX

OTHER BOOKS AVAILABLE IN THE 'HEAR MY VOICE' SERIES

Birmingham	Volume 1
Bradford	Volume 1
Croydon	Volume 1
Cumbria	Volume 1
Devon S/E	Volume 1
Dorset	Volume 1
Ealing & Hounslow	Volume 1
Essex	Volume 1/2/3
Gateshead & North Tyneside	Volume 1
Hereford & Worcester	Volume 1/2/3
Hertfordshire	Volume 1
Highlands	Volume 1
Hillingdon	Volume 1
Humberside	Volume 1
Kingston-upon-Thames 1994	Volume 1 (Adults and Children)
Kingston-upon-Thames 1995	Volume 1 (Adults and Children)
Norfolk	Volume 1
Northamptonshire	Volume 1
Oldham	Volume 1
Oxfordshire	Volume 1
Richmond-upon-Thames	Volume 1
Sandwell/Walsall	Volume 1
Sandwell	Volume 2
Sefton & St Helens	Volume 1
Sefton	Volume 2
Sheffield	Volume 1/2
Solihull	Volume 1
Somerset	Volume 1
Stockport & Tameside	Volume 1
Suffolk	Volume 1
Surrey	Volume 1 (Adults and Children)
Trafford	Volume 1
Wiltshire	Volume 1
Wirral	Volume 1